*Love You Abigail . . .*
*Always Did*

*By Ethel Gorham*

LOVE YOU ABIGAIL . . . ALWAYS DID

SO YOUR HUSBAND'S GONE TO WAR

# Love You Abigail . . .
## Always Did

ETHEL GORHAM

DOUBLEDAY & COMPANY, INC.
GARDEN CITY, NEW YORK   1978

ISBN: 0-385-13643-9
Library of Congress Catalog Card Number 77–11778
Copyright © 1978 by Ethel Gorham
Printed in the United States of America
First Edition

FOR DEBBY AND JOHN

*and JEAN*

*Love You Abigail . . .*
*Always Did*

# 1

I arrived in Paris late that Saturday evening, after a hideous crossing from London.

"Go by plane," Debby had insisted, before she herself left for Canada after her sabbatical year in England. I had come over to be with her for her last ten days in London, as part of my own holiday. I was set to leave the following morning for Paris.

"That Dover-Calais crossing is a stinker, Mother," she admonished me as we said good-by. "Really, don't do it."

I had never made the boat crossing before, and I didn't think the plane flight was all that convenient. If you added up the crush at Victoria for the airline bus, then Heathrow—that most muddled of airports—and the other waits and delays, the one-hour actual flying time to Orly counted for less than a fourth of the total trip.

"Furthermore," I said to Debby, "it sounds so twenties taking the boat train. I'd like to try it." In the back of my mind was the difference in price, too, but I didn't mention that, because it was the kind of penny pinching that irritated her.

So I stopped in at the travel agency on Heath High Street and arranged for the boat train. Early Saturday morning the taxi to Victoria railroad station came immediately on call. An accommodating driver helped me down with my luggage. I settled back happily in the cab and watched Hampstead disappear behind me.

"I'm off," I thought.

But I wasn't. Of all mornings, there was a derailment at Victoria. We drew up to the station to find people bursting out of all the exits, scrambling for cabs, attacking my taxi as I tried to pay the driver.

"Derailment," was the cry. "Everyone is going to Charing Cross. It's a mess."

"Derailment?" I hesitated, not dismissing the driver. "But I'm catching the boat train." My confused words bounced off the clamor of the crowd trying to get into my taxi.

"Listen, love," said one woman, "there's no boat train out of Victoria. You can take our word. You'll get one at Charing Cross."

I didn't know the rail system. I don't know London. I turned in bafflement to the driver. "Is there a boat train from Charing Cross?" I asked him, suddenly his face the one friendly familiar one in that whole mob. After all, he was on my side, since I hadn't yet paid him. "Or should I go into Victoria to inquire while you wait?"

He decided quickly. "Stay right here, love. Let whoever you want ride with you. It's Charing Cross for you, I think."

"We're going too, can't we ride with you," came the cries from outside.

"There's room for four more, if you want, madam," said the driver, so four others joined me, luggage piled on us all, and we inched through the traffic from station to station. Finally, with running and sliding, following one of the taxi passengers turned guide, I was on the train to Dover.

However, my guide had neglected to tell me that Dover Station is not the boat-train station, so again, with pushing and pulling and waiting on queue, I was misdirected to the wrong marine wharf, missed the ferry, and finally arrived, seven hours later via Hovercraft, and not the boat train at all, at the Gare du Nord.

It was eight-thirty. Abby was to have met me at six-thirty. I looked everywhere but she was not there. My luggage was unwieldy, there was no one to help, I felt like a fool. The crowds in front of the station were enormous, hundreds and hundreds, waiting in line for a taxi, fed through the funnel by a cordon of police. It took more than an hour, pushing my luggage in front of me as we inched along, before a taxi was mine. At last I was headed down to the south end of the city and the hope that Abby wasn't still somewhere in the Gare du Nord looking for me.

When the taxi drew up in front of her little building, she was at the window on the second floor, leaning out and watchful. Her lovely, anxious face hung over the iron grille, lit in the dusk from the light in the room behind her.

"Mummy, oh, Mummy, where in hell have you been?" she called down. "I've been out of my head."

"I know." My head was out the taxi window, looking up at her. "Oh, darling, I'm so sorry. I'm so glad to see you. Come down, help me with my god-damned luggage."

I heard her clattering down the stairs, and there she was. So beautiful, black cotton dress tight at the bosom, full-skirted above her ankles, showing bright blue stockings and black wooden clogs.

"My darling, my darling." I clutched her. "What a day! Not like F. Scott Fitzgerald at all."

"Mother, you're such a fool. I've been so worried." She hugged me fiercely while the dark-skinned Algerian driver waited impatiently for his money, not raising a finger to help us after opening the trunk.

"Let's get rid of him, shall we," we both agreed and yanked the luggage out of the trunk and out on the walk. She looked at my awkward suitcase, my camera bag, my big bulging shopping bag. She shook her head in disbelief.

"You'll never learn, Mother, never. No matter what I say. All this silly luggage."

I looked at her sheepishly. "I know," I agreed, "but I *am* planning to stay a month, you know. And the stuff in this shopping bag is some groceries and stuff Debby left behind."

"Groceries!" she exploded.

We hauled the bags together up the single flight of stairs to her studio. She insisted on handling the big one herself.

"I told you to take the plane," she chided me as we came into her place. "I can't forgive Debby for letting you go by boat. I did it at Christmas. It's a disaster."

I collapsed on her couch. It was so good to be in place. "Don't blame Debby. She warned me too."

"I'll make tea, something hot. I have some mint tea." She was bustling around her little stove. I looked at her. I had not seen her for nine months. I took such pleasure in her beauty. I never failed to respond to its headiness.

Tonight her long brown hair, caught at each temple by a tortoise barrette, was flowing down her back as I loved it—

because then I couldn't see the curve of her spine. She had a poetic, lyrical face, almost medieval yet sharply modern: wide-browed, pointed chin, enormous gray-blue eyes, sculptured cheeks, and then that marvelous mouth—full, sensuous, extended lips, firm and incisively curved, large in dimension, splendid when she broke into one of her big laughs—like a triumphant burst in that chiseled face, all her white, perfect teeth showing.

"I hate my mouth" had been one of her teen-age complaints. "It's so terrible. It's so big and *pink*." She went through a phase of trying to blot it out with the flesh-colored lipstick that was once the rage of Italian movies. I had been happy when that passed.

In those teens, Abby had been one of the most enchanting girls I had ever seen. She had a beauty that often made her self-conscious and unhappy. "I don't know why everyone turns to stare"; she would come into the house weeping.

"Maybe if you didn't wear those orange stockings and all that makeup . . ." her father answered dryly.

"It doesn't matter, Daddy," she protested through her tears. "No matter what I do, everyone stares."

It was true. With or without orange stockings, with or without makeup. There was a haunting radiance that made heads turn as she walked down the street; once, a boy of ten came over to our table in a restaurant in Italy and just stood there and looked and looked, his own eyes wide.

That was the year we traveled together, Abby and I, to Athens and Istanbul and Naples, and found our life made intolerable by the crowds of men who followed us and stared.

"The custom of the country," we mumbled to one another; "what a bore!"

Now, at thirty-two, her beauty had changed. She no longer had the ravishing, ethereal, madonna-like, aching look of her sixteenth birthday. Her face was seasoned and womanly; the wide, laughing mouth had become lusty and sensual, pink and generous without lipstick; the planes of her face were no longer like smoothed ivory, but hollowed and shaped. Her wide-spaced eyes beneath strongly drawn brows were steady and discerning. She was a lovely woman.

I leaped up from the bed toward her, to kiss her directly on those firm lips. "Abby, Abby, I'm so glad to see you." I clutched her closely. She held me as tightly as I her, arms around one another. "I've missed you so."

"Oh, Mummy—and I you. I was at the railroad station at five-thirty. I was so excited. And when you weren't there, I was sick. So anxious. Oh, Mummy."

She wiped the tears from her eyes with her sleeve. "That Debby," she covered up her confusion. "She should absolutely have prevented you from taking the train."

I pushed her back to look at here, even while I held her. "I told you. It wasn't Debby, darling. She was as insistent as you. It was me. But I'm here now." And drew her close to me again as we clung together.

We both knew our joined fear for one another. We were interwoven in the same texture of pain and loss. Charles had been dead now for ten months—her father, my husband—but Abby and I still suffered our mourning; and our tight grasp of one another was a way of saying how strong was that grief, how much we depended on one another to share it.

"Tea in a minute, Mother," she said and turned so I wouldn't again see the tears in her eyes.

I stretched out on the bed once more and felt my fatigue at the endless, frustrating day disappear. I looked around her studio, at the paintings on the walls—stark, exciting, dominant. Most of them, I had already seen when I had come to stay with her after Charles's death. Now I noted the two new ones. She had written to me about one of them. Her idea had been a painting of Zeyer's, the café at the corner of the Rue d'Alésia and the Avenue du Maine, where we always ate, where she always ate, where she and Jean went constantly.

Abby's work this last year reflected her strong, imaginative, personal involvement with reality. Her vision was dynamic, quirky. I loved the Zeyer painting. I told her so. "It's great, Abby, you've really done what you intended."

She stopped fussing with the tea. "You really think so, Mummy?" Her face was serious, sober, as it always was when we talked about her work.

"Yes. I love it." I got up and walked to the painting, standing directly before it. "I think you're on your own here. I really do."

There were about ten paintings hung around the walls of the studio, all in the same technique, with the same vision, the same eerie, direct perception of reality. I looked at each painting carefully, then at the whole. It was a created whole, a world imaginative and unique, completely her own.

"I wish you would think about a show," I said. "I know you were opposed to it the last time, but after all, there is no other way for an artist, is there?"

She had been opposed to a show the last time I had talked to her about one. She had even marshaled a number of reasons against signing one's pictures. Some philosophical bias based on opposition to the commercialism of the art world. Her answer now indicated another viewpoint. "A show?" She hesitated, then nodded. "I don't know. Maybe."

I knew this was a commitment. A positive declaration.

She flushed. She flushed easily. When touched or hurt or irritated or uncertain, she always flushed that way, deeply, the neck turning red first and the color spreading to her hairline. When she was a child, we had had her tested for more than a hundred allergies; against this reddening, against sudden inflammations and itchings, against what she liked to roll on her lips when she learned how to say it: *giant urticaria,* unexpected hives. Now, when she flushed that way, she had her own diagnosis.

"I'm allergic to myself," she would laugh. "I'm allergic to being pleased, mad, gay, put down, built up, loved, hated."

I crossed the room and hugged her again. "I love the way you look," I said, changing the subject, deciding to discuss an art show later; "what a great dress!"

Her mood changed, away from the stern contemplation of the work on the walls to her bubbling gaiety when it had to do with things. What delight she took in things! Not any things. Her kind of things. Now she twirled around the room in her clogs, making a brisk clunking noise.

She held out the wide skirt of the dress. "But look at it. You bought it for me, Mummy. This is the black sailor dress I wrote you about. I bought it out of the Christmas money you sent me."

She ran to her little closet and opened it. "See? And this—and this—and look at this." She held up a blue cotton jumper, blue the color of cornflowers, of a bird's blue wing; French blue, she called it. "Don't you love it? Isn't it the most bluey of blues?" She hung it back in the closet. "You were so right to suggest that I spend my Christmas money in London when I visited Debby. Everything is cheaper there." She patted her clothes lovingly as she pushed them back behind the closet door. "I adore everything I have. My friends say how do you manage all this and I say, *'Ma mère, c'est toujours ma mère!'* "

I stood there looking at her so radiantly grateful, and all I could say out of my overwhelming urge to love her and protect her was, "We'll do some shopping in Paris, too, darling. I was going to bring you something from London this time but decided to wait so you could choose it yourself."

As I sipped my tea, I thought of the gift I had indeed bought but did not bring. I had given it, at the last minute, to Debby.

"My daughters," I thought wryly, "both in their thirties, but they might still be three and nine, for all their need to be the favorite, to be loved by gifts, singled out. I should have known, from my own experience, that it never ends. Somehow, I had expected my daughters to be wiser than I."

We had gone shopping, Debby and I, because I wanted to buy her something to take back to Canada with her. She had agreed.

"I'd love a dress to start off the semester," she had said. "Less kooky than what I've been wearing all year in London. Something respectable for committee meetings."

We went to a favorite place in Knightsbridge, filled with racks and racks of cottons and teeming with young girls and young women buying them by the armful. Debby found what she wanted and then urged me to get a ruffled long skirt in a pretty wallpaper print.

"What do I need it for, honestly," I protested, "it doesn't make sense for me." She coaxed me, and because the skirt was charming, I agreed.

Then I said, "you know, I don't have a present for Abby. Why don't I buy her something here, a jumper or a dress, to bring to her in Paris?" I flipped through the rack. "Do you remember what she bought at Christmas? I don't want to duplicate anything."

Debby turned cool and reserved. "I really don't know what Abby bought, Mother."

"But weren't you with her?"

"Well, yes, but I really didn't notice." She turned away and left me at the rack myself. I picked a jumper in the same print as my skirt and we had the packages tied up separately. Debby was apparently upset and unhappy.

We crossed the street to a tearoom and ordered. Debby drank her tea quietly, her eyes downcast. I had no idea what had triggered this disquiet. Then she told me. Struggling with her own honesty, she confessed that she had been jealous at Christmas because my gift to Abby had been larger than her own.

"But, Debby, my darling," I tried to protest. I didn't know quite what to say. I wanted to blurt out, "How childish," but I didn't. "Christmas is Abby's birthday," I reminded her instead. "It was a birthday gift as well."

"I know, Mother, I know." Her face reddened and her eyes filled with tears of self-reproach. "I realize that. It's silly, I know. I just wanted to tell you because I'm so sorry about it. I'm sorry I was such an ass—back there, in the shop."

I shook my head. "Don't worry about it. I should have realized. No one ever gets over that childhood shit. It goes on to the end. My fault for mixing up the Christmas gifts."

Debby reached over and held my hand. She looked so vulnerable, her hair long and clean, cut in sharp bangs across her forehead, freshly washed each day; her unpowdered pale skin still spattered with freckles across her nose as it had been long ago, her intense beauty unmarred by any artifice. My dear daughter, I thought, professor at a university, who needed to be loved and loved and loved and who returned love and love and love like the spill of a constant waterfall, confessing to envy because her sister had gotten four dresses to her one. "Her panda," I remembered, "is bigger than mine"; I had been furious with my sister about it for half a century.

I squeezed Debby's hand. "We all have to learn, don't we, darling," I said.

"Me, too," she replied. "But I'm glad I told you. It's so silly of me, but it's me."

When we returned to Debby's apartment in Hampstead, I asked her to try on the dress bought for Abby. Just to see how it looked, I said. And because it looked wonderful on her, I urged her to keep it. She protested, but I protested back.

"Honestly," I assured her, "I prefer to have Abby pick out something for herself in Paris. It's better that way."

"Are you sure? Really sure?"

"I'm sure."

So here I was in Paris empty-handed. I set down my teacup. "We ought to think about food?" I suggested.

Abby sounded anxious. "Do you suppose we could go out?" she asked. "Are you too tired? I could try to cook something here."

"No. Why don't we go to Zeyer's. They're open late."

Abby sighed with relief. "Would you mind, Mummy? I could make you something here if you really didn't want to go. . . ." her voice trailed off. I was hungrier than her "something."

"Let's go. Come. I feel fine."

We walked arm in arm toward the Rue Didot, then up the Rue d'Alésia toward the brasserie—talking, talking, Abby talking mostly, wanting to fill up the gap of the last ten months with news of her friends, her surprises, her wonderments. It was dark. All the shops were closed, but it was familiar ground and my energy had returned after the tea and rest at the studio.

"By the way," she said as we pranced along, "I've seen Monique again, I've been meaning to write to you. Fantastic. You'll never believe it, she invited me to lunch and then arrived in a chauffeured car." Abby pulled at my arm like a child. "A chauffeured car, Mother, would you believe it? How idiotic!"

Monique, who was Abby's age, was a young woman she had known for many years. They had been close friends when Monique had married an old and famous painter. "And, Mother, the chauffeur was not even a proper chauffeur, just a young guy in blue jeans and Monique had him run around the car to open the door for us. It was out of a Truffaut movie."

Abby and I stood on the deserted street and roared with laughter.

Then Abby shook her head in regret. "I'm so sorry for Monique. She's absurd. But I'm sorry for her."

"But why?" I asked. "This has all been quite a good thing for her."

"But, Mother, think. She's just my age and he's over *eighty*."

I snorted. "Well, he wasn't exactly a boy when she married him, ten years ago. And she did love those long mink coats and all that fame."

Abby shook my arm. "You're so unfeeling. Things change. They've both changed. That's why I feel sorry for her."

"How have they changed?" I asked skeptically. "He's still making fabulous sums of money with his work and she still loves luxury."

Abby pinched my arm. "Don't be crass, Mother. I'm really sorry for them both. He's just painting himself, over and over again. He's locked into giving the galleries what they want, more and more of the same. He's boxed into his success. He can't do anything different from what has made him his money for the last twenty years."

"Other artists have managed to change their styles when they wanted to," I said coolly.

"Okay, Picasso. But he wasn't sucked in by the need for money. He made it, but I don't think he needed it."

"I suppose it is a problem if you desperately need chauffeured cars, clothes, expensive restaurants, big studios here and in New York. All of that just costs a lot."

Abby nodded. "The art dealers are the ones who are really rapacious. His dealers won't allow him to change the size of his pictures, because they say his public thinks of him as large, not small. Isn't that silly?"

As we rounded the corner toward the door of the restaurant, Abby added: "It's Monique I worry about. She's taken a lover and that's enraged him, but still, what is she to do?" She finished her thoughts after we were seated at a little table at the window. "But a lover isn't enough. It's so temporary. It worries Monique. She feels that she won't have any assurances of her life at forty. No certainty."

I shrugged. "That's asking a lot. How can anyone make certain—of anything?"

"But," said Abby, and there was affection and concern in

her voice for her friend. "What if he dies, what will happen to Monique?"

"More to the point," I answered her, "what will happen if he lives and lives and lives?"

Abby laughed. "Oh, Mother, you're impossible. So callous. Let's order."

We sat in the restaurant for two hours, eating amid a flow of words, back and forth. A hungry interchange, as if there would never be enough time to get caught up. And naturally, in spite of my determination not to mention Jean on this trip—we talked about him too. His name was constantly on Abby's tongue. It was inevitable that I should respond. She was so full of what he said, his ideas on this and that, his questions, his answers, his attitudes, his difficulties.

Jean and Abby had been lovers for seven years and I had never met him.

"Why not?" I had asked her again and again. At first, she had insisted that he was marginal in her life. She wanted no family involvement. Then, later, she became belligerent about it.

"Why?" she retorted when I spoke of it. "Why should you meet him? What difference does it make?" Sometimes she responded calmly, icily—sometimes in irritation, flushing from neck, chin, cheeks, up to the forehead.

The idea of a meeting between me and Jean obviously made her unhappy and uncomfortable. When she had come home, at the time of her father's death, there was a moment when we were in the kitchen together at the sink and I told her how much I appreciated her coming. I told her how important to me it was having all three of my children with me, how hard it must have been for her to manage it in such a hurry.

"Oh, Mummy, I wouldn't have not come for anything, you know that. Jean loaned me the money for the flight and he took me to the airport. There was no question of my not coming."

I was unloading the dishwasher, filled to the brim with the glasses that punctuated the round of visitors who had come to call that sad week. I thought for a moment and then responded to Abby deliberately. "I really would like to meet him, Abby. He is so much part of your life. After all," I wanted to forestall her protest, "it is not that unusual, you know, for me to want to know him. You talk about him so much and I'm not entirely deaf and dumb."

She was silent for an instant, as if weighing a truculent answer as in the past, then changed her mind. "I know, Mother. You're right. There's nothing unusual about your wanting to meet him. But I love Jean very much. And I love you very much and I just don't want to take a chance on the two of you hating one another. I couldn't stand it."

It was enough to silence me that moment. I did not want to create any confusion. I didn't want to pursue it. And one part of my mind accepted her point of view—what difference did it really make whether the situation was usual or unusual? And who was to say?

This time, as she talked about Jean, and with the prospect of my stay in Paris for a whole month, it seemed absurd that we should somehow be ducking one another for four whole weeks.

"I hope," I said gingerly, "that perhaps Jean and I could meet, have dinner or whatever, this trip." She stiffened. I put my hand out across the table and held hers. "It would really be more natural for us if this were so, Abby."

To my surprise, this time she nodded. "I know," she said

rather sadly. "I know. Nothing would give me greater pleasure than for the three of us to be sitting here eating and drinking and talking together." She pushed her food around on her plate, eyes downcast, thinking. "Okay. Maybe so. We'll see. Maybe when we get back from Burgundy." She sighed. "He's having a crisis now. It's the crisis of turning forty." She shook her head. "But then, there's always one crisis or another. Either me or him. I'll talk to him about it. Let's wait until after our trip."

The trip to Burgundy had been on our minds since last year. When the apartment in Paris was offered to me for the month of August, we decided to take some time and make the trip part of my holiday. Our plans were sketchy. We had written one another about setting off as soon as I arrived, within the next few days. Abby's friend Claude, who taught at the Beaux Arts in Dijon and knew the area well, had arranged an itinerary for us back in November, sitting at her little pine table and tracing out the route on a piece of white paper, complete with the best places to stay and eat.

"Semur-en-Auxois," he had insisted, pinpointing it on the map. "That's where you must stay." He scribbled the name of an inn on the paper and the name of the proprietor. "Tell Madame I sent you. She'll take good care."

Abby had kept Claude's directions, and we now intended to use them. Neither of us wanted to be away from Paris for too long, but we did want to get to the country together.

"Oh, the country, what joy!" she had written in June; "we've been struck by the worst heat spell in a hundred years and I'm parched for the sight of the country." But a letter following had warned that she could not take more than a few days away from her work. Our compromise was to plan a short trip, no more than seven days, departing whenever it suited us, with no fixed reservations, no fixed time of return.

We could have sat chattering all night at Zeyer's, but the waiters, who all knew Abby, always greeted her warmly, now stood in a cluster joking at us and making gestures about closing time. It was late. Paris is an early town. The night spots have their own, dawn closing hours. But, mostly, Paris shuts up early, and it is only in the brasseries that one can eat and drink past midnight. Then they shut up too. It was time to go.

Abby and I went to the corner, where she insisted on taking the taxi with me to Marie-Claude's apartment. I protested. I was worried about her return later, by herself, to her own place.

"Don't be silly, Mother. I do it all the time. I'm not afraid. And I want to get you properly installed in the place. You don't know it at all."

If I had arrived in Paris on schedule and as planned, we would have driven directly to the apartment from the Gare du Nord with the luggage and been free of it. Now it was a problem, still at Abby's place. We decided to forget it and pick it up the next day.

"You don't need anything," she said, settling back into the cab after giving the driver the address; "you'll learn how to travel light this way."

I knew how anxious Abby was to get me settled. I knew the special pride she took in having made this arrangement for me. It was her gift. All of it—the apartment, the trip together, the month that stretched ahead—was to be a time of healing for us both. She had written, "There will always be a hole in my life without Daddy." I felt her tenderness. I leaned over and kissed her cheek.

"Thank you," I said. "I'm so glad to be here."

The taxi drove up the ramp of a blatantly modern complex of buildings, with staircases marked A-B-C-D-, take left ramp for odd numbers, right ramp even. Then the elevator A for even floors, elevator B, odd. Somehow, in Montparnasse, it seemed especially lumpish. It was as if the ugly, aggressive Montparnasse tower had spread its influence into the whole quarter. Everything was landscaped, everything numbered, everything clean, everything as plain and ordinary as Co-Op City in the Bronx.

Abby opened the door of J 10, 2 F, and we were there.

"Is it all right, Mummy, is it all right?" Abby's voice was so apprehensive, she took these things so seriously, she was like a child bringing offerings.

I threw my arms around her. "It's marvelous, darling, simply wonderful. Imagine! My own place for a month."

There was a little living room, hung with batik, bells, plants, magazines, and books everywhere, a young friendly clutter. In the bedroom, there was not an inch to move around in, with its large double box-spring and mattress, its crib, clothes piled high in every corner. A kitchen, a bath—clean. The rooms were small but the comforts complete. The wide windows absorbed the lights of the Paris-Sheraton across the street.

"Abby, I love it. Wonderful." I hugged her. "You don't know how glad it makes me."

She was so happy at my pleasure, so relieved that I was satisfied, that she whirled around the room. "See, Mummy, see how clean it is." She led me into the tiny kitchen.

"Clean, I'll say it is. Oh, Abby, I bet you came over and cleaned it."

She laughed, that great, big, deep-going laugh. "What a

day I had! It was a pigsty this morning, a garbage heap,"
she roared. "They left in such a hurry. And anyway, you
know Marie-Claude. She never notices anything. She's a
slob, my favorite generous slob. I love her."

"You spent the whole day cleaning?" She knew I would
have wanted it clean; she and I are neat. "But I could have
done it myself."

"Oh, never." She lifted the lid of the garbage pail for em-
phasis. "See? Empty. The first time in years. And see the
fridge"; she held the door wide open; "clean, some food in it
too, good food. Marie-Claude says to eat and drink whatever you can lay your hands on in the place. It's all for you."

Abby showed me how to work the coffee grinder and we
made some for ourselves, fresh and strong and black. We sat
and smoked and drank it, reluctant to end the evening. On
the wall was a water-color sketch of one of the new group of
Abby's paintings.

"Marie-Claude liked it," Abby told me, "so I gave it to
her. She wants to buy the oil, but you know, I'm not ready
to sell—not that one or any of them. Not until I'm through
with this phase."

"I agree," I said; "you ought to keep everything if you are
planning a show."

She lit a cigarette and dragged hard at it, filling the room
with the acrid, delicious odor of the Gauloise. "I'm afraid of
showing, I guess. Not because I'm not sure of myself. I'm
afraid of the commercial pressure of the galleries. It's too intense, too vindictive, finally non-productive. I've seen it with
friends of mine."

"But we always come back to that same question. How
else can a painter get known? How else make a living?"

"I don't know. I really don't know. The art world in Paris

is such a mess. It isn't your work that counts. It's the publicity impression you make. The kind of personality you are. Baudelaire's green hair. And that awful word *in*."

"Is it better in New York?"

"I don't know. New York is the critics' town. The reviewers are more important than the painters. They write all that turgid nonsense, they have no ideas that can be helpful to the working artist. Their only effect is to create the crowds at the museums. Art and circuses. The young painter gets lost in the computer count at the gate."

She was silent for a moment, squinting her eyes through the smoke, a habit of hers. "No, the critics have no effect on artists—or on the future. They just add to the excitement of the gallery goer, who then goes to as many as three or four big retrospectives in an afternoon. Unbelievable.

"And the crowds!" she continued. "They hardly look at the pictures after they get there. They stand in front of a complicated and beautiful picture and chatter about the last visit to the dentist." She shuddered. "I read about the hordes at the Metropolitan, but it's as bad here in Paris. Remember last year's Jacques Villon show at the Grand Palais? And remember the tour guides, each in another language, each with its own group, at the top of their voices, bedlam."

She shook her head. "I don't know how a painter survives. I really don't know. Yet maybe it would be a good thing for me to have a show. If that's the way it is . . ." her voice trailed off, questioning, yet regretful too.

"Perhaps I can help you," I said. "I don't quite know how. But anything. There are people I know who might be cooperative in Munich. Alice has a friend who has a gallery. Munich might be a good place to start."

"No, no." She shook her head. "Paris, Mummy. This is where I work. This is where my friends are. I'm not interested in Munich—or New York—or anywhere else. Just Paris."

Paris and Abby. People in France were always surprised that we were mother and daughter. It baffled waiters and strangers.

"But you're French," they said to Abby, "how come—your mother—?"

Abby spoke French as a Frenchwoman. I limped along, my French fluent enough but obviously a second language. She took joy in the way she spoke—yet almost never, when speaking English, did she introduce an unnecessary French word. She found each tongue sufficient unto itself. She had an innate delicacy about it, a respect for each language; she could manage to say what she had to say in one or the other. "*Oeuvre!*" she would shudder. "A critic's word. A foreign word. Why not *work?* A man's total work?"

Abby's Frenchness was an important dimension with her. It was both interior and exterior, a certain way of being. Once, a few years earlier, she had taken a job as a film animator in a studio near Les Halles. I called for her there one evening after work and we walked to the bus at Châtelet for the return home.

As we crossed the bridges toward the left bank, the whole panorama of the Seine spread before us—the medieval and legendary towers of the Conciergerie, the great width of water busy with boats and barges; the crowds, workaday crowds, going home at this hour from the long hard day, walking the bridge toward the subway; the tower of the Horlogerie looming in front of the bus, the marvelous blue of the clock luminous in the night light—and I said to her,

"What do you think, what goes through your head, making this trip every day, over this historic route, seeing it as a commonplace while for me it is a visitor's delight?"

She answered me with a rush, eagerly, passionately. "I think I'm the luckiest person in the whole world to be living here in Paris now, this very minute and crossing this bridge twice a day on my way to and from work, and to be close to people at the studio that I love."

It had been a hard winter, that one. A time of money difficulties, personal estrangements, pain. I had wanted to help her financially, but her father had been against bailing her out.

"The last thing that would be good for her would be to get money from home and be like every other American in Paris, sitting on her ass in a café, waiting for the check. She can work. I work. You work. You'll be doing her no favor by subsidizing her."

That was his point of view. He may have been right. Or not. I went along with him; our only gifts to her were clothes and books and records. So she got a job. At the film studio she was surrounded by friends and companions who helped take her out of the depression and lassitude that stemmed from her personal problems. And her joy on that bus ride across the bridge St. Michel came from belonging to Paris as all those others did, as part of its blood stream, its working force.

Abby was a French citizen. She had married Philippe at eighteen, and even with their separation and divorce, she retained her French citizenship. Because of it she never felt expatriate. If she was ever homesick or nostalgic, it was only for her childhood, which she remembered as the happiest in the world.

"Not until I was seventeen," she once said to me, "was I ever, ever truly unhappy. Not even with that whole terrible business of the curvature of the spine and our rushing from doctor to doctor. I just took for granted that Mummy and Daddy would fix that too. I never expected anything else."

It was now almost three o'clock in the morning as we sat talking about art shows and Paris and Munich and New York. She looks drawn and tired, I thought, it's late, my first night in Paris, but we have a whole month ahead. "You'd better go, dear. Look, see how late it is." I urged her off the couch and to her feet. "Unless you want to sleep here."

"Oh, no." She stretched and yawned. "I like to wake in my own place."

"Isn't it too late for you to be out alone?"

"Don't worry. There are a million taxis down below."

We embraced and said good night. Our plan was to sleep late the next morning, Sunday, and to meet at her studio for lunch. Leaning out the window after she had gone, I was cheered by the sight of the cabs filtering down the avenue, to and from the Montparnasse Station. I told myself that, of course, she had found one without difficulty, although I could get no glimpse of her. I was disturbed and uneasy. The coffee, the cigarettes, the fatigue, the talk. I drew the blinds on the windows and tried to shut out the light of the Paris-Sheraton below.

# 2

---

I was tired, but I found it difficult to sleep. I had had an extraordinarily long day; what a day! from Hampstead through Victoria, Charing Cross, Dover, Calais, Gare du Nord, and finally Abby. And all that miserable luggage. I laughed in the dark. She was right. I never did know how to cut down. And then, whatever I brought was never quite right. Oh, well. I tossed and turned. It was a hot night; the windows open behind the curtains brought in the ceaseless noise of the boulevard. And in my mind, constantly in my mind, Abby.

Had she found that taxi easily and was she safe at home? That was comforting and immediate for me to worry about. But I always worried about her. Was her back better? Worse? Hard to see. She carried herself like a dancer. She was tiny and supple, and from the front, beautifully shaped. When her hair was down, long, over her shoulders as it was tonight, the distortion of the spine was not visible at all, although I looked for it, tried to see it, like worrying a wound, poking away at an aching cavity.

I sighed into the night. How wonderful that black cotton dress looked on her, I thought—you'd never know, never. The thought comforted me. She had learned what clothes to wear, had worked out a formula through trial and error. When the scoliosis first became evident, it was late, she was in her teens. I tried to buy her loose-hanging, chemise like dresses with no waistline. She became angry, hostile.

"Mummy, they're like maternity clothes, I just won't wear them. What do I care what I look like from the back? I can't see."

After she was married to Philippe, he agreed with her and insisted I fussed too much. He even insisted that she not go for the check-up examination the doctor had recommended be made when she was eighteen. I knew what was in his heart, in hers too: if one didn't admit it, perhaps it would all go away.

And since she was married then, making her own decisions in her own, headstrong way, that check-up was never made. Did it matter? How did I know, this hot, hot night? One doctor had said, at sixteen, no surgery. Another had said, immediate surgery. The no-surgery doctor was the more eminent and the surgery sounded so drastic, we all decided to let it ride until the check-up at eighteen.

"We'll see, let nature take its course," the eminent no-surgery man had advised us. "Come back in two years."

So eighteen came and went and nature did indeed take its course. When Abby and Philippe were separated—they were then both living in New York—she agreed to see a man from the Hospital For Special Surgery. What a bastard that one was! He predicted a wheel chair at thirty, crowding of the heart and lungs, the direst consequences. All this in a cold way, in front of us as if we were objects, pointing to the X rays lit up behind him as if they alone existed and we—Abby and I—were the spear carriers in the wings off stage, waiting for the star and the director to cue us forward.

He had a Greek name and spoke with a Brooklyn accent. "Immediate cracking and resetting of the spine," he drooled over his litany, "two years in a cast. Then another cracking and resetting of the rib cage." And then? No, there was no guarantee of success.

Abby listened, her face sober and attentive, like a student's, as she leaned forward to catch each word. Then, clearly and distinctly, she said, "Fuck that," and walked out of the office. I trailed behind her, making polite noises at the doctor, while his jaw hung loose for a moment in surprise. I saw, as I trailed Abby out of the room, that he simply turned off the lights on the X rays, and I heard not a word out of him, not a human word.

Abby and I took the subway back to her studio, which was then on Spring Street, holding one another's hands. It was noisy on the Lexington I.R.T., and the shuttle over to the West Side rattled. Neither of us wanted to talk. But, once we were out of the subway, heading for the turn around Sixth Avenue, she announced: "I'm going back to Paris to live. I can't stand the dimensions here."

She was then twenty-four years old and a very successful illustrator. She had saved some money, managed to squirrel away enough after Philippe's excesses to make her mobile, and had, as she said, no intention of devoting a decade of her life to a chancy chance on a straight spine.

"Anyway," she said firmly, "I want to paint, the way I did before I started all this illustration shit. You could go on

being top dog in this advertising and magazine business all
your life and all you'd have would be money."

What a lucky move that was, I thought, what luck! After
Abby had been in Paris a year, I ran into a German doctor
with whom I talked about scoliosis.

"But your daughter lives in Paris," he said. "They are
doing marvelous things with that problem there." He gave
me a name to investigate. I did. When I called the French
woman who had headed the department at the Hospital for
Crippled Children, I explained that I had a daughter living
in Paris who was no longer, alas, a child, but could something be done?

Her reply on the telephone was clipped and precise. Had
my daughter ever had surgery?

"Unhappily no," I answered.

She was a woman of seventy, I had been told, but her
voice tinkled merrily on the phone, young and eager. "Happily, then, because we don't take patients who have *suffered*
surgery." She chuckled. Obviously, she looked forward to
the challenge of competing medical practices.

The result of that telephone call had been, if not miraculous, at least astonishing. Abby was started on a series of
medical exercises, performed in the clinic set up by the doctor, that worked wonders. No cure, but no wheel chair either. Pain alleviated. The process of curvature arrested.
Even some important correction.

It was explained to both of us during that first interview
in the clinic, that the French look upon this curvature as a
malformation of the muscular structure. Others, in the
United States for example, see the process as a malformation
of the spine itself. If it is muscular malformation, as the
French see it, then the way to handle it is to re-form, re-

educate the muscles back to normal. No one had ever spoken to us this way in America. If there were doctors who accepted this form of treatment, it had not been our good fortune to find them.

Abby went consistently for the exercises: in the beginning she had gone four times each week; now she was down to two. It was a long trip for her, all the way to the Trocadéro, with a tiresome change at the Montparnasse Station. I once asked her for how long. Abby replied simply, "Forever."

"Other people go to yoga twice a week, Mummy," she had said when I winced. "This isn't so very different."

The cost of all this, which Charles and I had assumed in full at the beginning, was now carried partly by the French health system. We had felt that, whatever it cost, we would pay. We felt it was part of our parental responsibility, in some deep unmentionable way, our fault.

Guilt. That awful wash of guilt. Should we have spotted the scoliosis earlier? No one was looking. We'd never heard of it before. Our respected and popular pediatrician didn't see it until her teens. I tossed around on Marie-Claude's low, big bed, listening to the zap and zoom and warm-up of the motorbikes down below, the big buses arriving and departing, even at dawn, at the Paris-Sheraton across the way, the tangle of early Sunday-morning noises, and felt that sharp pressure around the heart that always came when I thought about Abby.

Ah, yes, that black cotton dress, it was delicious on her. My mind returned to it and the bright blue tights, the little black clogs. She wore the most marvelous clothes, clothes from the flea market, muslin petticoats for dresses, little velvet capes. Jean had given her a little opera cape that had belonged to his grandmother. She wore it with blue jeans and high boots—and no one ever looked at her back. Except me.

"How frail she looked!" my mind insisted on worrying through the night. But I knew she wasn't frail. She sometimes looked vulnerable and helpless, but I knew she was strong-willed and determined and powerful in her drive for life and work. I knew she smoked a lot of pot. I knew she experimented in a variety of ways with love and life, but none of this worried me.

What worried me? Was it my enormous need for her, my feeling that she was so integral to my life that any possibility of risk to her hung there in the background of my being? Not in my mind, but behind my mind, behind my thoughts, somewhere in the veins and the arteries, the nerves and the muscles, lurked my fear of losing her.

A wave of acute anguish swept over me as I tossed through the hours, wondering if I had been right to come to Paris at all. Charles's death was too recent and too overwhelming. When I had been here directly after his death, staying first with Debby in London, then with Abby in Paris, it had been different. I was encircled by their love, they guarded me, Debby and Abby, putting off for me the inevitable return to the lonely house. We shared a formal, traditional enclosed time of mourning, our own kind of sitting *shiva*.

But this summer trip was another matter. We were supposed to be on holiday and I wondered if I was ready for it. Perhaps I needed more time back home, in my own house, learning to grow accustomed to widowhood, before I ventured into outer space.

"Stop it!" I said angrily to myself, "stop fidgeting. Try to get some sleep." My reason told me I worried about Abby even when I wasn't in Paris. I never stopped. But here, in her own life, her graphic presence, the sympathy between us, the rush of understanding, the closeness of mind and body, made my anxiety more acute and stripped my nerve ends.

I finally fell asleep and didn't awaken until eleven in the morning. I could hardly believe the time. I was normally awake hours earlier. I dragged myself through the kitchen, weary with the long tossings and the drugged hours that followed it. I tried working the little coffee machine that Abby had so carefully explained the night before, and gave up at my clumsiness. There were tea bags and some *biscottes* and a bit of jam and I began to feel better.

I looked out the window. A sunny day. There were crowds in front of the hotel, so many in uniform—airline pilots, stewardesses—and enormous sight-seeing buses drawn up to the front, at the curb, waiting to load or unload, I couldn't tell which. Over the reaches of the new buildings were the derricks and cranes and cherry pickers that filled the Paris sky above the rows of old houses still left to be picked and clawed and uprooted, tomorrow or the day after.

I bathed leisurely and thought Abby would not be displeased to have me arrive late for lunch. The thought of Jean crossed my mind. What a nuisance not to know how Abby arranged all this! I didn't even know whether he lived at the studio with her and disappeared for my arrivals or whether he had a place of his own. I had no idea about their arrangements at all.

"It would be damn gauche," I thought, "to get there and find him, before he had time to vanish." Then I thought mis-

chievously, "But of course that would resolve the problem of
our meeting."

I put that out of my mind at once. She had made such a
point of not bringing us together, it would have seemed
cheating to have it happen accidentally. No, it would have
to be quite formal, an arranged affair, not a break-in. But as
I thought over the days ahead, a whole month, I sighed, "I
hope this turns out all right. I really can't dispossess him for
a month."

Thus the fact that I was somewhat late this leisurely
morning didn't trouble me. I slipped into the slacks and
shirt I had worn all the day before. I thought I would drag
something out of my suitcase when I got to Abby's and
change there. I looked forward to lunch and whatever plans
we decided on for the day ahead.

Out in the street, the heat was immediate. The soaring
temperatures of the summer were now somewhat lessened;
the worst of the heat wave was supposed to be over, but the
hot air still struck the skin with a palpable blow and the eye
saw the city through vapor. The streets seemed locked in a
parched and brownish mist.

The Montparnasse subway station was just around the
corner, but I decided to avoid its labyrinthian passages and
walk to the next station instead. I crossed to the Avenue du
Maine and headed down. When I arrived at that station, Gaité, and looked at the subway map on the board
above the entrance, I saw there was only one other stop between it and the station I needed, Plaisance. It seemed
easier to walk all the way, so I headed down to the Rue
Raymond Losserand, then to Alésia and on to Abby's studio.
I noted that it was already past one o'clock, it would be late
by the time I arrived, but the stroll beckoned me on.

Early Sunday afternoon on Paris shopping streets is fun.
Even in August—and it's a myth that the whole city is completely deserted in August—there is the bustle of marketing
for the Sunday lunch, the little lines gathering now at the
butchers', the bakers', the cakemakers'. The shop windows
were loaded with platters of grated carrots and celery salad
and beets with peppercorns and onions. I was tempted to
buy as I passed them but decided against it. We'd buy together, I thought. We'd pick what we both wanted. And
though my head ached from the restless night, I was so glad
to be walking toward Abby, so happy this moment that I
was I, dawdling my way toward her, and she was there,
waiting for me.

A twist, a turn, down her street. There was the park she
had told me about the night before, that the city of Paris
was building at the end of her street.

"Such good news," she had announced with delight,
"imagine, a green park to walk in and sit in, fifty yards from
my place!"

Then she added, partly out of her own native acumen and
partly in concern for the investment that Charles and I had
made in the studio, "That will increase the value of this
place, Mummy, you know."

I looked at the big sign above the vast demolished area.
Yes. THE CITY OF PARIS IS CREATING GREEN SPACE FOR THE
NEIGHBORHOOD, it said, and was properly signed by all municipal leaders. The large enclosure was circled by a high
wooden boarding, but I could see through the slats. I was
pleased. "Of course Abby is delighted," I thought, "what a
nice thing it will be to have this little park here."

The purchase of the studio had been one of the more sat-
isfactory things that Charles and I had done together for

Abby. During her first years in Paris, when she had returned alone, she had rented one of those tiny new Paris boxes that pass as apartments. It was in a modern building, elevator and all, but the apartment itself was about the size of an orgone box. It had a bath, no kitchen. (Although technically, Abby had explained, there could be a kitchen. A shelf was provided in the closet on which the tenant could put a little two-burner plate and a tiny fridge, if it was bought by and maintained by the tenant himself!) The *main* room barely accommodated a drawing board and a studio couch.

Her letter, when she found the place, had been ecstatic. She was delighted to have it because it was cheap and modern and in an area she loved—only two Métro stops from Montparnasse. It was small, she admitted: when you walked into the room, a low-ceilinged, immaculate white cube, with shiny parquet floor and one whole wall made out of glass with a door on to the terrace (a terrace! she rejoiced), that's all there was. You were in it—and the place was full.

She had managed to bring her own charm to it. The walls were lined with painted orange crates in which were all her things, her little toy soldiers, her compositions of pencil holders and funny plastic shapes, old dolls and antique figurines, books and records. The couch was covered with pillows, her grandmother's crochet pillows, and the fake furry spread I had given her. Against the window wall that led on to the terrace!!! she had shoved her drawing board.

And how noisy it was! It was noisy within and without. It was so constructed that even the sound of the light switch in the adjoining apartment could be heard. Outside, every day, all hell broke loose. All the noises of the Avenue du Général LeClerc, the constant revving up of the cycles beneath her window, the crush of traffic on the narrow street leading to the avenue, with the shouts and imprecations of the drivers stalled in the crisscross.

She loved it at first, was delighted by its low rent, adored the area, where in an instant she could sink into the everyday Paris crowds—ordinary Paris, she called it, with its endless shopping queues, its flamboyant food stalls, cheese stalls, fish stalls, fruit stalls; with the carts on the avenue, the dress shops with exactly the same clothes as St. Germain, and at the same prices, too; the cafés where she went each morning for coffee and croissants (because, of course, she never bought the two-burner plate) and sat in the sun until it was whatever time to go back.

Yes, she did love that little place, but then she began to feel cramped in it. She had to admit the terrace was just big enough to stand on and look down when someone rang her bell; certainly too sooty even for plants. As her emotional strength returned and she really wanted to paint, it was too difficult to find the space. And finally—the last disaster—the threat of a raise in rent.

We talked about it on a number of my visits to Paris. I was uneasy about that little apartment. It seemed so confined. I knew that when she once more turned her mind around to painting, she would somehow manage to find a place to do it in. But this tiny cage seemed to me to be a way station, a delaying action, a small, charming impediment. It also troubled my conscience. I would look around at all my space in Connecticut and regret the meagerness of hers.

The irritation and ineptness of the apartment eventually got to Abby and she wanted to move. But the economic fact of life in Paris is that it is far better to buy than to rent. Abby was loath to face me with the problem. I faced her.

One spring, I suggested we go house hunting. Charles and I had talked about it over many months and decided, after taking everything into consideration, to borrow on his insurance and allocate the money for a purchase.

"Why wait until we're dead?" we both agreed; "that's no time to leave someone cash if it's needed now. And she does need it now. What's more, this is a permanent investment for her."

The house hunting gave Abby and me a jolt. Charles and I had thought we were being so bighearted, so princely. The money we offered was a drop in the bucket. We told a real estate man what we wanted to pay and he lifted his eyes in surprise. But he was a nice young man and he took us on the rounds to let us see what was available for our price.

He showed us a mean little room with no windows in one charming garden nook (I had specified charm, alas); another, with more space, was in a smelly old house with no toilet in the apartment, a w.c. two flights up; another, in a collapsing grand old house on the Rue de la Gaité, had a little railroad flat carved out of what had been one great room. Above the broken partitions, one could catch glimpses of the fine old moldings and the carved plaster ceiling. This had no running water.

We climbed stairs for three days, dodged many dogs, looked at one another with woeful eyes. It was apparent that what Charles and I had so carefully decided we could pay, would buy what was not worth having. Where did people get all the money?

There were only two days left to my charter trip and I felt the strain of frustration at our lack of success. But, behold, Abby knocked on my door early the next morning. I was staying in a small hotel around the corner from her place and I was surprised to see her so early, and in a state of great excitement.

"Mummy, the realtor says he has a *bonne affair* which isn't even on the market yet. It just came to him this morning and he ran right over to me. He wants us to look right away."

The real estate man was very amiable and eager. He drove us to the place, discussing all the good points in advance. The place was in the Fourteenth Arrondissement, Abby's preference. It was on a quiet street. It was in a good old house, somewhat *moyen,* said the young man, but solid and well maintained. In it now lived a man, a house painter, with his wife and three children. Very respectable, and so forth. He had just decided to sell, he was moving to the suburbs.

"The price?" I asked the nice young man, rather cautiously, knowing somehow that all this excitement so early in the morning, boded more than had originally been intended.

"Well," he answered just as cautiously, "half again as much, but worth it, wait until you see, and maybe we can shave it a little since we are the first."

Abby looked at me helplessly. I shrugged and made a decision, sight unseen. If what we wanted to pay would buy nothing worth having, perhaps there was wisdom in seeing what this could be. The finances would have to be analyzed later with Charles. Perhaps the insurance loan could be extended.

The building was indeed *moyen,* but solid and old, as the man had said. The entrance hall was narrow and a little turn of stairs led to the apartment itself. "Good," I thought, "not too much climbing."

The house painter's wife opened the door just an inch, to

look at us, then wider. Behind her were three quiet, staring children. We were led through a tiny narrow foyer into a small first room, which served as kitchen, bedroom, dining room, to judge from the furnishings. But—wonder of wonders—a high wide window over the sink, open on a tiny balcony with a beautiful view of a fine garden below. My eyes fixed onto the garden. I was enchanted. It was the first thing I pointed out to Abby.

She was firm with me. "That's not important, Mother. It's the inside that counts."

Very well. The inside was spotlessly clean, newly painted. Beyond the little first room, somewhat bigger than Abby's own place, was another, larger room with two tall windows, apparently the room for the three big-eyed children.

"You could throw down the partition and make it all one," I suggested.

"Do you like it?" she asked tentatively.

"Well, it does open on a garden."

"Mother, please, the garden hasn't anything to do with it. Concentrate on the work area I might have here. Don't mention the garden, please."

Later on, we called the garden the unmentionable. Once, she wrote me that "the unmentionable is not to be believed. I have my breakfast out on the balcony every morning. Next door is Vera de Silva's garden, with an apple tree with white flowers on it and an enormous lilac bush which I can see. It's very quiet out in back and loaded with blackbirds that whistle."

There aren't so many things that one does in one's life that one feels completely right about. This was. The purchase of the place gave Charles and me much joy. After it was done, the deed executed and Abby in full possession,

we sat and talked about it with a special happiness, grateful
that we were able to do it; it had meaning for us beyond the
fact itself. We felt that in some direct and forceful way we
had opened a passage to new possibilities in Abby's life.

It was so. She wrote, "You can't know. The studio makes
all the difference to me. I've christened it by starting a large
oil painting. I really could never wish for more."

Late as I was getting to her place that Sunday, Abby
wasn't quite ready. It was ever thus, I thought philosophically. But she looked exhausted from the heat. Her hair
was piled on top of her head, lovely and wispy, with strands
of it falling around her cheeks and out of the barrette onto
the nape of her neck. She wore the same black dreas as the
night before, the same bright blue stockings too, and the little black clogs. The rouge was high on her cheeks, and now
because her hair was high too, my eyes followed the curve
of her back beneath the sailor collar and I felt the familiar
twist of anxiety and regret.

"You're early, Mummy. I haven't been out to shop yet,"
she said as she hugged me.

"Oh, darling, it's hardly early. But don't worry. I'll shop
after I sit for a minute. I've walked all the way."

My eyes followed Abby as I stretched out on her couch.
She always suffered from the heat, and now the tension of
having me as a guest for a whole month must add to her fatigue. She seemed very pale beneath her patches of rouge. I
closed my eyes for an instant's rest and then looked around
the studio.

It was really not so big (and remember, I thought, five
people once lived in this space!), but Jean and a friend had
helped Abby take down the partition and turn it into one
austere, ordered space. Everything was impeccable, com-

posed. I noticed she had even shoved my alien suitcase and camera bag under the bed so as not to spoil the composition, her design.

"Up, up, old lady," I chided myself as I rose from the couch. "Give me a shopping bag. Everything is open on the street now. I'll get our lunch."

As we sat together on the balcony and ate sliced tomatoes, some cheese, some paté—chewing into those little reinette apples that are so sweet and so tart at the same time —drinking it down with watered wine, Abby peered down at the roses and sighed at the damage the long dry spell had wrought. She was proprietary about it all.

"I hope there isn't permanent damage to the trees," she said in a worried voice.

I reached over and held her hand.

"I know," she said, understanding my gesture. "This has been an oasis for me."

"I'm glad," I said. "I love it too."

There was, around the corner and down the Rue Didot, a small flea market on Sundays, at the Porte de Vanves. We both liked to wander about it and, the year before, I had bought all her pots and pans there.

"Why don't we go over to the market at Vanves this afternoon," she suggested. "It's something to do on Sunday and I know you love it."

"Just what I'd like to do this afternoon," I agreed. "It's nice and lazy."

"I'm looking for a good, wide muslin petticoat," she said. "Maybe we'll find one."

"Let me buy it for you," I offered eagerly.

"Oh, Mummy, no. If we find it, I'll get it. I can't mention anything without having you want to get it for me." She hugged me tightly, kissed me on the cheek. When she kissed, she really did. Her kisses were deep-going and delicious, suction kisses.

"But I didn't bring you anything as a gift."

"Oh, come on. Let's go."

The flea market at Vanves is minuscule but neighborly and fun. We walked around it arm in arm, exclaiming over a splendid oak armoire, which she poked at, opening the doors wide, running her hand over the wood sensually, in delight, fingering the ornate hardware, sighing at her desire for it; then an old felt hat that she plunked on her head and said, "I want it, I want it, it's just like the one that Daddo used to wear, isn't it crazy?" tossing it back onto the litter she had taken it from, shaking her head no, no to the long-haired, blue-jeaned boy whose cart this was; and then clapped her hands exultingly at a big spread of muslin underwear, old nightshirts and petticoats and chemises.

Her fingers tightened on my arm as she whispered hoarsely, "I knew it, I knew it, look at all these things."

We went through this stand wildly, looking for the petticoat she wanted, calling across the piles of underwear: "Look, Mummy"—"See this, Abby, what do you think?" Alas, there was nothing either of us wanted.

"Maybe we'll find what you want on our trip to Burgundy," I reminded her.

"That's right. You're right. We'll do better in Auxerre or Beaune. And everything's overpriced here."

At one of the stalls we ran into a young woman, an American that Abby knew and whom I had met the year before. She was selling off some of her own old flea-market clothes.

"I need the money," she said as she greeted Abby with a kiss on each cheek. "Look at all these wonderful jazz-age things. I hate to part with them." She shrugged, we shrugged back. The Spanish shawl, the fringed flapper sheath, the beaded chemise—they were all too expensive, they left us cold. Abby and her friend again embraced; we wished her well and continued our circuit of the market. Over the bridge and around it and over to the other side.

Suddenly a young woman ran over to us and touched Abby on the shoulder. A young, tall, handsome woman, very dark, elegant, blue jeans, black turtleneck sweater, wide leather belt with a magnificent metal buckle.

"Aren't you Abigail Gorham?" she asked.

Abby wrinkled her brow; she had a way of wrinkling her forehead and pulling her eyebrows together when in question. "Yes." She nodded. "Yes, but—" she clearly didn't recognize the other young woman.

"I'm Lorna Brown. St. Hilda's School. I thought I recognized you."

Abby looked closely. I did too, trying to see a fifteen-year-old schoolmate behind the Parisian flair.

"Lorna Brown?" Abby sounded uncertain.

"Yes. I was in the class behind you. That's why you don't remember me. But I do you."

"Lorna Brown. Of course, of course. What a thing, to run into you here!"

"I heard you were in Paris," Lorna said, "but I didn't know where."

"How long have you been here?" Abby asked.

"Six years. I'm doing graphic work, some layout, for a publicity place. And you—?"

"Seven years."

They smiled at one another, a confidential smile that enveloped all they knew of living and working in this city.

"Are you painting? I heard you were painting."

"Yes. And my studio's right near here."

"Let's get together. I'd love to see you."

"Yes, yes, wonderful. My mother and I are going in a few days for a little trip to Burgundy. When we get back." They exchanged addresses. Abby seemed enthusiastic at the encounter.

We left Lorna, again arm in arm.

"How nice she seemed," Abby exclaimed. "I'd like to see her again, definitely. And imagine running into two Americans in one day. I never do, somehow, from year to year. And St. Hilda's, my God. A million years ago."

St. Hilda's! Abby in her blue serge uniform. The Reverend Mother.

"Remember the Reverend Mother?" Abby said now, shaking me with glee.

"Remember her? She was unforgettable, an original."

"A type," agreed Abby. "A marvelous specimen of the *she*, herself."

St. Hilda's had been unexpected, inadvertent for Abby. We had sent her to Dalton, because it seemed standard in the framework of our lives in the city. But that so-called progressive school had demanded vagrant orthodoxies, up one day, off the next, that Abby had not been able to manage. Either she was the one caught smoking; or she wore the orange tights on the day they were prohibited; or she didn't please the painting instructor, who was, at that time "into" abstract and minimal art and intolerant of anything else; or she swiped the mercury from the laboratory because she was fascinated by the way it behaved in her fist—anyway, she was the one that raised the dander of the headmistress then in charge.

Charles was at home when the school called, so he went. I like to think I would have been more politic, but he sat tight-lipped at all the charges, which seemed absurdly trivial to him, then plainly cursed out the headmistress, called the place a gilded ghetto, and managed to sever relations for all time. After which, he returned home with Abby in tow, called the Reverend Mother at St. Hilda's and St. Hugh's, and asked for an admission appointment for Abby.

She spent two happy, involved years there. The Sister in charge of the art program had studied with Diego Rivera, and she knew, from Abby's work, how serious was the commitment. She respected Abby's attachment to the Art Students League, which had angered the teacher at Dalton. Abby had been attending the League after school and on Saturdays since the age of thirteen, when the scoliosis had first shown its curve and ballet school became impossible. The Sister put Abby in charge of the sketch class and allowed her the fifteen-minute leeway each afternoon to catch the Fifth Avenue bus down to the Art Students League for her class there.

The League, for Abby, had been Charles's doing. When it was clearly impossible for Abby to continue at the ballet school, I had wept in my room, enraged at the physical blow that had been dealt her. Abby had been one of the children in the cast of the first Balanchine *Nutcracker*," and she loved the idea of thinking of herself as a possible ballerina.

I anguished, but Charles acted upon it. He took her to the Art Students League within the week that the doctor had prohibited the ballet and asked her to look around.

"Isn't this fun," he said to her, as they walked from studio to studio, poking in the thicket of easels set up in each one.

"Why don't you try going?" he suggested. "There aren't

any rules, no obligations. We won't be stuck for any tuition if you decide it's not for you. We just pay from month to month."

She agreed, tearfully, uncertain, unhappy. She would try it. She chose Mr. Fogarty's class, worked hard there and became completely devoted, even electing to stay through one whole hot New York summer to act as monitor while others were on some beach or hillside camp. She told us proudly when she asked our permission to do it: "I'll be the youngest monitor ever. You know, it's an honor."

The Art Department at Dalton may not have approved of the League—too representational—but the Sister at St. Hilda's made no judgments. Work was work and learning was learning, and no one should impose one aesthetic over another.

Abby studied at the League until her graduation from St. Hilda's, when she went off to the Boston Museum School. Graduation at St. Hilda's! The Reverend Mother, starchy and preening over her first graduating class in the Cathedral of St. John the Divine. Abby in a long white tulle-skirted dress, which she never again wore—"My God, how tacky! only the Reverend Mother could dream that one up."

We chuckled at the resurrected memories of St. Hilda's as we walked back to Abby's studio down the Rue Didot. I reminded her that even given the Sisterly tolerance, they were often dismayed at Abby's behavior. "And no wonder," I said to her in that Paris sunlight. "You were a terror."

"No I wasn't." Abby shook her head firmly. "No, really I wasn't." She was quite serious, almost offended. "I just liked to talk to lots of people and listen to them, even if I didn't know them, and I loved wandering around upper Broadway."

The school was near Columbia University, and the Sisters had injunctions about going home directly. They were fearful of upper Broadway, concerned about their young girls. But injunctions? Taboos? Restrictions? These were never Abby's style. Her disciplines came from within her. They had to make sense to her. The only imposed restraints she accepted were those that shaped and made intelligible her work or her life or her loves.

She had once gone into a cafeteria on 103rd Street and Broadway, accompanied by two or three of her wilder schoolmates, also bent on breaking rules. They all discovered, after ordering their buns and cokes, that no one had money enough to pay the check. Abby said, "Watch out, I'll get it, no washing dishes for us," and approached a man at another table. She asked for a loan of a dollar, got it, and promised to return the next day to repay it.

I don't know if there was a gleam in his eye as the rendezvous for the next day was made, or if Abby had carefully selected the handsomest man around, or if it was all innocently uncalculated and just like Abby. But word got back to the Sisters; we were telephoned at home about the terrible tale of Abby picking up a man, soliciting for funds, and then lying about it to the Sisters when confronted the following morning.

Bless their good, nunnish hearts, those Sisters. When Abby confessed to me later that indeed she had borrowed the dollar, that if anyone in such a jam had asked her and she had had the money, she wouldn't have given it a second thought and loaned it, it seemed completely reasonable to me, and completely reasonable to the school—but for her own protection, Abby was forbidden the part of Broadway again.

Also, three demerits for fibbing to the Sister that morning and denying the tale!

Also the payment of a dollar, which Sister Angela was to return to the young man at the cafeteria that afternoon. The man turned out to be a Columbia sophomore, and I secretly chuckled at what must have been his surprise when the debt was paid by a black-habited nun.

Dearest Abby, said Charles and I to one another that evening, such a pain in the ass. Always involved in her own logic, always following her own, fairly innovative paths.

"Imagine!" said Abby now as we turned the corner into her street. "Imagine running into someone from St. Hilda's."

"It all seems so far away, doesn't it?" I said.

"No," she answered wistfully. "No. A million years away, maybe, but that's not far. It was all so funny good there."

Then she broke into laughter again, gusts of laughter, stopping in the street to clutch my arm with another St. Hilda's memory.

"Oh, Mummy, remember when Sister Angela took me to the ballet on Fifty-fifth Street because she wanted to share one of my special things with me and you gave me money to take her to tea after the performance and I took her to Sammy's Sixth Avenue delicatessen?" We both roared again.

"Well," said Abby defensively, "that's where we always went after the ballet, you and me and Daddo. I thought Sister would love it."

"But she did, Abbo, remember. She did."

"She was completely freaked out," Abby agreed. "What's a pastrami sandwich? she asked delicately when I suggested it—and that waiter explaining it. He was darling. Izzy. Our favorite man. You should have it with a glass of tea, he told her. And she did. With a glass of hot tea, lemon, although I know she wanted milk."

We stopped in front of a new apartment building near her house. The bushes in front had grown in the past year. The planting had been spare and bare, now it was an interlacing of green.

"I wonder what they are," I said. "Such a great ground cover. And so green. In spite of the drought."

"Want me to ask the concierge?" she said. "Maybe they're an idea for you to use back home."

"Oh, no. I'm through with all that. I wouldn't even put in a weed now. But these really look great."

Abby poked her toe into the edging of the bushes. "They're so close together, the dogs around here can't poop in them with any comfort."

"The dogs," I sighed. "It's as bad here as Brooklyn Heights."

"It's not as bad here as in the Sixteenth. Those dress-up ladies and their awful little dogs. They stand there and watch them poop, that's what they do, wherever their little dog hearts desire. And all those initials, on the ladies and the dogs. All those cheap plastic bags that say Vuitton and Dior and St. Laurent. Only, they don't say it; you have to be in the know. They ought to be made to put the dog shit right in those bags. That would be significant status, really symbolic."

The narrow little hall into her house was cool and I tracked up the stairs behind her gratefully. It had been a lovely afternoon, but the first of August heat was heavy. It was comforting to go from the street into the ordered, composed quiet of her studio. The brilliant outburst of color in her paintings struck me freshly each time I saw them. I thought they were wonderful. Gay and happy, vivid with life. Her work at the animated-film studio had influenced some of her shapes and conceptions. One painting had a group of black children on roller skates, skating across the canvas, one into the other, a continuum of motion, dazzling in design and color.

I stretched out on the couch, propped up by the mass of pillows, and looked at it with a surge of admiration. "How mature," I thought, "how fulfilled."

"It takes a long time to be a painter," Abby always said. "The greatest asset is a long life."

She was really started, on her own way. I looked at each of the canvases around the room. They were stunning, each one, all together. That one over the couch; I reached back, craning my neck to look at it again. It was the finished oil of the sketch now in Marie-Claude's apartment.

Art criticism, art talk, has a glossary with which generalizations can be made, a kind of verbal filing system to index the visual experience. Magic realism. Surrealism. Minimalism. Conceptualism. They are codified jargon.

This painting was an ordered, structured dream: a woman at a café table, demitasse in front of her, on her head a little hat with a crisscrossed nose veil, in the fashion of the early fifties. Flying toward her, aloft, from the right, was a young girl in her early teens in a blue cotton jumper, hair very black, thick bangs, straight across the forehead, bobbed abruptly below the ear. An odd, strange scene.

"The little girl is me, Mummy," Abby said fussing with the tea water yet watching me closely. "Don't you see?"

"And the woman?" I asked. "She has such a closed, set, efficient face. Is that me?"

"Oh, come on, Ma. It's not really you or me. It's just you

and me in another way." She came over and stood in front of me on the couch and looked at the painting. "I remember you when you worked with all that fashion jazz. The little hats. The little suits. So elegant."

"But the face is so shut tight. So proper."

"No, no. I don't think so. Just closed. Waiting for me to get there. See? I'm on the way."

"I see." I laughed. "Abby in levitation, late as usual."

"It's the Coupole, you know. Don't you recognize it?"

"Vaguely. But it doesn't matter, because it *is* somewhere. It's definitely in its space." I thought for a moment. "But it seems out of time. That's what makes it so troubling, a sense of fantasy. It's a time remembered. A time to be." I shook my head, disturbed, touched in the innermost way by the mood of the painting, the stillness within it, the suspended flight of the child, the locked-in woman.

"But do you think it's good?" she insisted.

"Very good. Very, very good."

"I'm glad you think so. It's important to me."

I knew that Abby took my appraisal of her work seriously. I don't know that she agreed with all I had to say, nor did I always agree with her—but we were serious with one another about serious things. And her work was one of them.

"I'd like to buy the skating picture," I said. "In advance of a show or later. I love it."

"It's yours," she said. "Come onto the balcony. The tea is ready."

We sat on the tiniest balcony in all of Paris, with its minuscule iron table and two tiny chairs. The speckled green-and-white leaves of the fusain down below glimmered in the afternoon sun. There was a single large reddish-pink rose high on one of the trellises on the fence.

"I'm so glad there's at least one rose for you to see. They were devastated early on this year."

We breathed the air deeply and reveled in the quiet. I stretched comfortably. "What a pity it seems, to take off for our trip right now, when I've just come. It's so heavenly here."

She sounded concerned. "Oh, do you really not want to go, Mummy?"

"Oh, no, no." I didn't want to disappoint her. But was she afraid of disappointing me? She had seemed happy and expectant of this Burgundy trip in her letters home, but I wasn't absolutely sure it wasn't for my sake. And it *was* comfortable here. There was all of Paris to wander around in. Still, she had seemed eager for the country. "I didn't mean not to go at all. I just thought, if you'd like to put it off until later in the month . . . ?"

She thought about it, looked through the window of the balcony into her studio and at the unfinished painting on her easel: three big, heavy-faced men, three patrons at a bar, traced on the canvas—coarse, metallic faces, the faces of prosperous butchers. She squinted. "Maybe, then, if you're not in a hurry, we won't go tomorrow as planned. If you really don't mind, Mummy, I'd like to put the background on that one; then it will be dry when we return."

I was eager to be even more accommodating. "But, honestly, dear, next week is good too."

Again she thought about it, then shook her head. "No, why don't we go as planned, but let's put it off until Wednesday, if that's really all right with you. By next week Soizette will be back in Paris and some other friends too and it will be good to be around when everyone is back. You'll enjoy it too. No, let's go now, this week, on Wednesday. Let's make it definite."

So we made it definite. We brought out the little page of directions that Claude had marked for us. National 5 out of Paris, skip the autoroute, down to Auxerre, then to Avallon and about three miles below Avallon, to the left, a side road to take us to Semur-en-Auxois, where we could stay. A marvelous Gothic town, said Claude, and a nice inn. Not expensive. Good food. He said to use his name with Madame. I had a road map and clipped Claude's directions to it.

"Okay," we agreed, and I folded up the map. "I'll take this to look at some more and I'll rent a car for Wednesday morning. How's that?"

"Done."

It was late afternoon. I could see that Abby was tired. I, too. We had walked to the Vanves, around the market, and back. It was tiring enough for me, but I knew how it must be for her. Even with the medical exercises, which now permitted her to walk good distances before feeling the pain in her back, she tired easily. Especially in the heat. I decided, after tea, to take the subway back to Montparnasse so I could rest in the apartment and she could lie down here on her own couch.

"But no," she protested, "I want to help you back with your luggage."

"Let it go," I said. "We can do that later on. Or tomorrow."

"Are you sure?" She was tired, I could see.

"I'll go on." I embraced her. "Shall we meet for dinner?" The question was tentative—inside that question was the question of Jean.

"Of course dinner," she answered firmly. "We'll be

starved. But not too early, eh? Shall I come pick you up at eight-thirty?"

"See you, dear love."

"Bye, Mummy." Again that lovely, suckling kiss on each cheek. "See you."

# 3

At the apartment, I filtered through the pile of magazines next to the bed and dozed and read. I was uneasy about the planned trip to the country, reluctant to leave Paris, where I had not had a place to myself—aside from a hotel room—for years. It was so good to be comfortable, on my own, yet with Abby as the pivot. I would call my own friends soon, make some luncheon dates and arrangements for dinner; but, for now, I wanted to engulf myself in her. But did she really want to go? Was she doing it for me?

I was restless. I read a long article in the *Nouvel Observateur* on what had happened to the leaders of '68. I put it down impatiently when I had read it through. What indeed had happened? Exactly what had happened to the New Left of the sixties at home. All swallowed up by academia or domesticity or business or all three. The kids at Nanterre, the kids at home—some kids.

I changed magazines. This time, I was enveloped in

glossy, full-page photographs, great wastes of space, a dou-
ble-page spread of one girl, all skin, on a single speck of St.
Tropez. Enormously dull. I tossed the magazine away. What
a waste of color and pages and time! Silly.

I dozed, then woke with a start. It was dark outside. The
lights of the hotel opposite were bright in the sky, flashing
and winking through the heavy heat. From the window,
Paris had a deep-night look. What time was it? My heart
started to pound, I could feel it pumping, poom, poom
against my eardrums. Abby, what had happened to Abby?
In a panic, I leaped up to the door to see if the bell worked,
and when I rang, it clanged through the apartment. I closed
the door with a bang.

Abby? Where was she? I couldn't tell the time on my
watch without my glasses. My glasses? I had tossed them
down impatiently with those magazines. I fumbled in the
heap. Those damn glasses; where were they? "Dammit," I
thought, "I spend my life looking for those glasses." I found
them and finally focused on the time on my watch. Not
quite eight o'clock. But why so dark? "Ah, that Paris double
daylight time," I remembered; but I sat there still shaking.
What in hell was the matter with me? Abby, who was usually late, wasn't yet late. Calm down. Why so jumpy?

I knew. I thought I knew. "It's Charles, I thought. "It's
too soon, too soon." Paris smelled of youth and love. The
afternoon at Vanves had been so gay and happy; everyone,
the two friends that Abby had run into, all so young, so full
of themselves. And I was still in grief. "I am bereaved," I
thought; "I am the bereaved." It was too soon for me to
have made this trip. Too soon to be in a strange apartment,
alone. I wasn't ready.

I knew I would be calm again someday. I had watched so

many of my friends left alone. What were the statistics about women my age? For most it would be widowhood. We all knew the statistics. There was no choice except acceptance. But no one talked of death. The loneliness descended, the pain was swallowed. Death, the actual death, was a forbidden subject. The terror was interred with the bones. One had to take it *well*, be strong, be silent.

Death of a loved one, Camus had said, clears the air, exposes a whole terrain unseen earlier, opens a way to a new landscape. We understand, he said, that the loved one obstructed a whole corner of the possible, pure now as a sky washed by rain. I tried to think about it that way, to absorb it. But generalities, like statistics, are only tolerable philosophically. This was my husband who was dead—my husband, who had been my comrade, my friend, my antagonist, my challenge, my despair, my delight, for almost forty years. What new landscape was there for me?

I wanted to be home in Connecticut, in the house that was filled with his reverberations, benign and enfolding, talking to him as I still did, feeling his presence from room to room, asking such ordinary questions of him: what about the furnace, the roof? I trembled now with the sharp desire to go through my own front door, close it, lock it, and be there, enclosed by the other life I had not yet relinquished.

I stood in the darkness of Marie-Claude's house and wept. What was I doing here in Paris?

The night Charles died, I'd had to cable Abby. She had no telephone, nor did most of her friends. It was not until the next day that I heard from her. When I told her of her father's death, she sobbed quietly, wordlessly. When she spoke, her first words were, "Now you'll come to live in Paris, Mummy, won't you? You'll come."

I was silent for an instant on the phone. So strange. Ten years ago, fifteen years ago, there would have been no question. Of course Paris. Now I could not answer Abby. "Can you come home, Abby dear?" I said, leaving her question in the air. "Is it possible?"

"Of course. But think about it, Mummy, think about coming here to live."

"We'll talk when I see you. When can you come? Debby is here now from London, and John arrived last night from California."

"I'll get the first plane I can, of course."

"Do you have money? How can you arrange it?"

"Don't worry. Jean is here and Soizette too. Everything is cool." Suddenly her voice wavered. "It's only my passport."

"Your passport?"

"Oh, you know." A bit of embarrassed silence. "I let it lapse. And it's Saturday, the consulate is closed."

"Abby," I thought. "Just like her. A lapsed passport over the weekend!"

But she managed, as she always did. She arrived—and there were my three children together for the first time in years. We were the caricature of the nuclear family, that hateful phrase. We had exploded in time, dispersing particles thousands of miles apart. One day inseparable—with all the problems such closeness entails—and then, bang, a shot spun round the world.

Was it only death that could bring us all together again, me and Debby and Abby and John, come to mourn Charles? But here they were, so dear, so close, all of them, close and warm and intimate. I felt encircled. No, I might never go to live in Paris or L.A. or Ottawa, but I was glad they were there, returned to me when I needed them.

I jumped when I heard the doorbell ring and stumbled in the dark to open it. It was Abby, of course. Abby still in that lovely peasanty black dress, her hair down to her waist, her face smoothed of fatigue, aglow in the pale light from the hallway lamp. I stood there looking at her, blocking her entrance. Her eyes were made up, each lash stark and clear, and there was pale violet shadow on her lids. But the pink on her cheeks was barely noticeable and she wore no lipstick. She was ravishingly beautiful and I drew her close to me, inexcusably emotional, so glad to see her, so relieved. She hugged me back, engraining that deep kiss on each cheek.

"What are you doing in the dark, Mummy?" she chided, pushing me out of the doorway and into the room. "Really!"

"I was asleep," I mumbled. I had no intention of telling her of my panic, my inundation of despairs. "I just got up."

She looked at me closely and understood. "Get dressed, why don't you? I'm starved."

She pushed me toward the bathroom as she whirled around the room. She pounced down on the couch, next to the stack of magazines. "That Marie-Claude! Look at this assortment. The *Nouvel Observateur* and *Elle* and all these knitting magazines—and see this new book *L'Ange* that everyone's talking about and Mailer's Marilyn Monroe. What a heap!" She pushed them aside. "Come, Mummy. Shall we go to dinner? Let's see what's open the first of August."

I stood there shaken, feeling dismally old. "What shall I wear?" I said tremulously. "My stuff is still at your place."

"Wear? Wear anything. Wear something crazy of Marie-Claude's."

I turned to go to the bathroom. Suddenly I felt better. "I'll get washed. Something crazy of Marie-Claude's indeed.

I'll stick to my same slacks. But tomorrow we must pick up my luggage."

"I know. I'll help you. We'll get it over here tomorrow."

"Anyway," I called from the bathroom, "it probably bugs you to have it there, interfering with the décor of your room."

She laughed and called back to me. "How did you guess? I know I'm slightly mad on the subject. I don't like anything out of place."

My face felt better after the cold-water wash. My eyes were still red and swollen; nothing to do about it. I dashed some of Marie-Claude's cologne on my neck and arms. I enjoyed experimenting with other people's smells. I slipped into the same black cotton slacks and top that I had left London in. "I'm not the same as you," I grumbled to Abby as I did. "I like to change."

She smoothed down her dress, fingering the cloth lovingly. "I take this off when I work. And I like to wear the same thing day after day until it gets dirty. Especially when I love it. Then I don't have to think about it."

I ran the brush through my hair. "Still, it will be fun to see you in those other things you bought in London. That blue jumper."

"I promise. Come on. Time to go."

"I look scruffy," I grumbled, looking down at myself.

"I love scruffy-looking women of a certain age, hair all on end, long earrings, tacky-looking, interesting clothes. That's what I want to look like when I grow old."

"That's not me," I sighed as we closed the door behind us and rang for the elevator.

"Oh, no, not yet. You've got some leftover chic. You're like me. We'll both get rid of that one day, you'll see."

There was a Moroccan restaurant on the Rue de la Gaité that Abby suggested. We walked that way. "Jean and I love it. I hope it's open. The food is extraordinary. And the décor is superb, Valentino in *The Sheik*." But it was closed: FERMETURE ANNUELLE.

She was so disappointed. She made me peek in the window to see some of the blue-and-white tiles on the walls, the Moorish hangings, the burnished copper pots suspended from the ceiling.

"Isn't it incredible?" She squeezed my arm in her excitement, shivering with a kind of personal ecstasy, as she did when she was enchanted by a thing or an idea, as if she would burst with it. "Isn't it wonderful? Oh, I'm so sorry you can't see it."

The closing sign listed the reopening date, September 3. "Oh, dear, you'll be gone. I'm desolate."

She looked desolate for an instant, then made me read the menu still clipped to the window within. "Too bad, too bad." Her arm went around my waist as she steered me away. "But you'll be back. Next time for certain, we'll come. You'll love it."

We wandered around the corner to the little park and the fairly good restaurant on its edge, but it was crowded and we had made no reservations. We decided to go to Montparnasse, corner of the Rue de Rennes, to Chez Rougeot, which was always open and always good. So, arm in arm again, one shoulder into the other because we were the same height, we pushed our way through the evening crowds of Montparnasse.

At the corner of the boulevard, there was a large circle around a street performer, everyone clapping and shouting, children out for the summer evening with parents, darting

in and out between the grown-up legs, or standing wide-
eyed, bewildered and bewitched by the spectacle within the
circle.

"Let's look," said Abby. "Oh, look, it's the fire-eater. I always love this. It's so corny." She was entranced, it didn't
seem corny to her at all, this street performance she must
have watched a hundred times. She followed the flaming
torch with eyes open in disbelief, fascinated. She gulped
when the great flames disappeared into the young man's
mouth. She grabbed my arm and whispered, "I wonder how
he does it. I really wonder how he does it."

We each gave a franc as he passed his hat, and Abby
sighed because the spectacle was over.

"That's what I'd really like to be," she said as we watched
the traffic across the wide boulevard and edged our way
through the pedestrian walk outlined with its shining hob-
nails. "I'd like to be a mime or a fire-eater or an acrobat.
And wear a clown's hat and have great patches of rouge on
my face and a big red nose."

I laughed at her delight.

"Come on." She caught my wrist. "Duck that taxi. Here
we are."

The Rougeot is an enormous, turn-of-the-century restaurant, the large room in the rear all *fin de siècle* lamps, the
walls lined with Art Nouveau decorations in tile, etched
frosted glass separating the center row of banquettes. The
few tables in the front share some of the back room's splen-
dor, with mirrored walls and *torchères* on the partitions. It
is all quite authentic of that Parisian era that touches the
heart the most; very noisy, not too expensive, and very
neighborly. The choice tables on a warm night like this were
on the terrace outside, under the awning, in the full blast of

the street's traffic but also with full view of the passing pa-
rade. We were delighted; there was a vacated table as we
came in, and the waiter signaled us to it. We settled down
in the corner, cozy and noisy and relaxed.

"Aren't we lucky," we congratulated ourselves, unfolding
the large white linen napkins. "We made it just in time! I
love it on the terrace."

The waiter, as old as the restaurant, barely able to hear us
in the uproar of street and diners, took the order from Abby.
When we were together in France, it was Abby who always
did the talking, almost as interpreter, to my chagrin. I once
told her that this annoyed me.

"I never get any chance to speak French in Connecticut,"
I protested. "And it isn't that bad, you know."

"I'm sorry, Mummy," she answered, "your French is excellent; it's just that the waiters always seem to look at me."

It was true. She looked as if she belonged. It was natural
to turn toward her. She patted my hand. "I was determined
to let you do the ordering this time. It's just that that old
waiter can hardly hear."

I patted her hand in return and we sat holding hands
until our wine arrived. We were always very physical with
one another. We kissed and hugged and held hands and
walked arm in arm. One night, some years earlier, in St.
Germain, a group of young men had whistled back at us—
"Quelle ménage"—and I had been startled enough to pull
my arms away from hers.

"Salauds," she called back to them, laughing, then pointed
two fingers toward the leader, "ta gueule," and pulled my
arm back to hers. "Don't pay attention, Mother. Don't let
them force you to change your step. Never. Not ever."

We had a lovely dinner, eating it slowly, enjoying the terrace. Abby ordered the herring in cream, then an enormous meat dish of lamb and white beans, later a salad, coffee. I, the usual fish that I adore in Paris: trout with almonds.

"I hope this isn't all too expensive," she said as she put down the menu after ordering.

I reassured her. "I've been working. And I intend to spend every single penny on our time together. So eat, my child, eat," I mimicked my own mother.

She ate like a trucker and never weighed more than a hundred pounds. She had such a huge zest for her food that it was not only the quantity she consumed that made it visible, it was the manner, too. She gulped and pushed and shoveled the food in.

"I know," she looked at me with a wry smile, "I'm a disgrace," as she mopped up the sour cream of her herring with a heel of bread, pushing the whole piece in her mouth at once. We had tried, when she was a child, to do something about what we called her table manners. "But, Mummy," she had wailed, "this is the way I enjoy my food." As she grew up, she tried to reassure me: "I don't eat this way when I know I shouldn't. I only do this with those I feel comfortable with. Honestly, I know the difference. When I'm in proper company, I don't disgrace you. I prove I'm well brought up indeed."

"Come on," I had protested, "how can you switch back and forth?"

"Of course I can. I switch. We all switch on everything all the time. When I'm comfortable, I love my food this way. Gulp, gulp, gulp, like Porky the pig."

While she ate through this meal in her true trencherman fashion, we talked.

"I didn't like London," she told me. "It was really an odd,

odd Christmas for me. I loved being with them. I love Debby and Chris and David, but it was odd."

"Odd? How?"

"Well, I don't quite know. Perhaps the difference between London and Paris. Or between the academic and me. I felt so out of it. Like an intellectual flyweight with all those brains. Debby's friends are so bright, so good-looking, but booksy. And I'm not a flyweight, you know." She suddenly sounded rather hurt and pugnacious.

"Flyweight, Abby? Hardly! You're one of the most articulate and considerable people I know. Debby knows that too."

"Oh, I know. In real terms, yes. But it's not Debby, really —although I suspect she doesn't feel that I always react in exactly the right way, especially with her friends. I'm not obviously scintillating, in that special way." She sighed. "We went to this party in Hampstead and everyone was extremely nice, but I felt they disapproved of the way I looked —of how I talked—or maybe of how I didn't talk—of me.

" 'So Parisian,' one dame said, as if that were poisonous. And there was this terribly pretentious and bubbly young man, so full of himself, who told me he was in something called "Upstairs, Downstairs" and I had to ask him what that was, which seemed to be some sort of *faux pas*." Again she sighed. "I still don't know what it is. No one ever said."

I laughed. "It must have given him quite a jolt for you not to know. It's just one of those big, well-known current successes on television—in America, too. But there's no reason, really, for you to know about it. Just to reassure you, Debby told me about it and she thought it was a howl. She was amused you took him down."

Abby raised her eyes in amazement. "She was?" She

sounded pleased, relieved. "Well, really. And I thought I
had goofed." She was silent, in thought for an instant,
weighing whether or not to speak. She lit a cigarette nerv-
ously before she did.

"Another thing, about Debby. You know, Mother, I was
very upset. Like a fool, I told her about the Christmas
money you had given me and your suggestion that she take
me shopping in London. When she heard how much you
had given me, she was livid, angry, deeply affected. I could
have bitten my tongue for telling her, but it was done. I'm
so sorry. It never occurred to me not to."

"I know." Debby's sad and troubled face last week, when
she told me about her jealousy, flashed through my mind. I
had not intended to mention it, but now that Abby had
spoken, I decided to let her know that Debby had told me
about it and what she had said.

"I don't think Debby realized it was your birthday money,
too," I began.

Abby interrupted in protest. "But she has so much,
Mummy. She earns a fat salary; what difference does a hundred dollars mean to her? I couldn't understand it."

"It hasn't anything to do with money, Abby. You know
that. And Debby does, too, because we talked about it."

"You did?" her voice rose in surprise.

"Yes. She told me what a heel she felt for being spiteful
about it."

Abby's eyes filled with tears. "It isn't that she's spiteful.
No, no. I never thought that." She lit another cigarette and
puffed at it intently. "It's just so late in life for either of us to
hold onto old hang-ups. You and Daddy always gave me this
Christmas birthday money for clothes and things. And you

know how generous Debby always was with money to me. I could count on her when I needed it, always."

"Yes, I know." I was silent, thinking about it. This was a painful residue in our mutual memories and I felt a sweeping wave of pain and regret. It went back to the time when Abby asked for an allowance while in Paris and Charles refused it. Debby had been forthcoming, creating an opposition, a kind of juggling of relationships which had hurt me, even as I was glad it happened. It had been an act of love and hate. If it deprived us of the authority of parental generosity; if it served, at that moment to signify Debby's antagonism to Charles and me and our feckless difficulties; it had revealed the deep concern of the sisters toward one another.

Abby shook her head thoughtfully. "I love Debby so. But sometimes I think she doesn't quite approve of me. I think sometimes she has romantic notions of what it means to be an artist and she tries to encourage me in them. But how can I tell her, being an artist is being a workman, a hard-working workman, and it isn't romantic at all. It's standing every day at that easel. Or over the drawing board. And then the results are so unpredictable."

"You mean the success, the rewards?"

"No, not only that, that's another source of worry, of anxiety. But it's the unpredictability in the work itself. It doesn't evolve according to the inner eye. You have to return to it again and again. At least, I do. I make so many drawings before I start a painting. I toss around, thinking about it. I approach it and retreat and then suddenly, it's marvelous, I'm at it, into it—but just when I think I have it finished, I don't know. I'm sure, I'm not sure. I love to work, I'm a workman, but a romantic! Oh, no."

More coffee, more cigarettes. It was late, so no one was eyeing our table, waiting to dine. We were free to stay. Abby went on thoughtfully.

"As for gallery success. Well. You know Roy. I love his work, quite original—and he does well, he sells, a lot of notice. But he has to make himself—he, himself!—into a part of the show. It isn't only his work that has to meet the eye. It is Roy, as object. He must go to all the exhibitions, get around, display himself. He threatens to dye his beard. Maybe purple, for oneupmanship." She laughed. "Why not? I bet it would look great on me. I'd love purple hair, I'd be a purple cow."

She shifted back to Debby. "Debby worries about the way I live. She doesn't understand when I tell her I intend to live marginally all my life."

"Marginally? Don't you mean unconventionally?"

"No. I really mean marginally. On the edge of things. It isn't simply that I don't want to get married. No one gets married these days. But Debby worries about my future, my well-being, my life. It is not even a matter of how well I eat and dress. I love good food and you know how I love clothes. Just a few things, not much. Just what I want, if I can. No heavy luggage." She leaned over and kissed my cheek impishly.

"You and your generation, you worry about this kind of thing don't you?" she asked me. I shook my head in disagreement, but she went on. "When your dear friend Myra came to see me last winter here in Paris, she said, so lovingly but so obtusely, 'If only, darling, you could find a man as wonderful as Chris.'" Abby exploded. "As wonderful as Chris! How does she know the kind of man I want? She knows I have Jean. Why should I want anyone else?"

I tried rather feebly to explain my friend. "She means well," I said weakly, then I agreed with Abby. "Did she really say that? What a dumb thing to say!"

Now that Abby had gotten this bit of irritation out into the open, she tempered it. "Oh, I don't want to criticize Myra, Mother. She's your dear good friend and it's wonderful you have her, but really!"

Again I tried to be defensive. "Well, I've nudged you sometimes too. Remember I once said, 'I'm looking for a nice Jewish doctor for you!'"

Abby broke into loud laughter. "But I knew you were joking. God, a nice Jewish doctor! Just exactly like Daddy! But Myra meant it, because Chris is a darling, and what's more he's a professor." She chuckled, the explosion over with. "Chris is charming and a good poet, too. But no one, not anyone in the whole world, should ever assume to know what another person wants or needs." She shook her head emphatically. "No. My last word on Myra, Mother. If you don't mind my saying so, and she's charming and fun and warm, but she hasn't a clue to what it is not to be exactly like her. Sympathy, so much. So tender. But empathy—well, no, not really."

She folded her napkin carefully, quietly, in thought. "I tried to make Debby see what I mean. Living marginally. I mean it in the sense of not going along with what goes on in the middle, in the mainstream. Not even what goes on in the mainstream of art.

"That art mainstream is poisonous; it has been polluted by those who bathe in it, wallow in it, swim in it for all the wrong reasons. It's like taking a cool clean river and mucking it up with beer cans and cigarette butts and scum. It's all the more contaminating and harmful than rejection, it seems to me. Think of the social power in owning the works of certain artists." She shuddered. "It's dreadful. People become *in* because of what they've bought. And the social power of the art critics, who swell up on their own words and cultivate their own prestige."

She suddenly looked dejected and forlorn. "I'm not sure I can ever take that or make that. I'm not sure of myself socially, in that way. You know that. I can't even come into a big room filled with people without trembling. All that smell of money and that expensive rose and jasmine mixed with musk, it really rocks me. And the talk. I can't understand it. I can't match it."

I had seen her become tinier and tinier, shy, like a little girl, uneasy, when faced with a razzle-dazzle of people. In her own way, under her own steam, she was witty and gay and at ease. So profound and then so funny. But she closed up like a flower, silent and still, when bombarded by alien chatter. Her face would redden, she wouldn't join in the conversation; she listened and could be caustic about it later; but she hid within herself when she wanted to hide, curled under her own wings against the buffeting chic.

It was not only Debby who worried about her vulnerability. So did I. And her father, too.

"She's tough, Abby is, as an artist," he once said. "She's determined and stubborn. But she has to come to terms with her own skill. She's a marvelous craftsman. Very deft. Imaginative. She has to grow into her skill. Too much praise when young. She has to develop the fortitude to match it." I remember he shook his head sadly. "There are certain things about Abby that are outsize. She has to learn to manage them. Her beauty, sometimes she wants to display it, to flaunt it. She exaggerates it in her clothes, her style. Other times, she wants to disappear."

I remember how sad he looked as he added, "And there's the question of her back. She hates the fact of it. And she's afraid of it. And she doesn't admit that there's never a moment without pain. It does something to you, that sort of pain." He spoke quietly, from his own torment, his own years of constant, harrowing pain.

I looked at Abby as she signaled for our check. It was hard to imagine the conflict, the wounds, the turmoil beneath that romantic, enchanting look.

As we waited for the check, Abby began talking again about Debby. "She worries about all the wrong things about me. Take pot, for example. You know I've been smoking since I was seventeen." I winced inwardly at the statistic. "At one point, last year, I had heard so much about it being dangerous and interfering with the ability to work—*Le Monde* had a series on it—that I decided to give it up. But I had a big stash in the house. Why throw it out? I decided to keep it, not to smoke it. An experiment in addiction, you could say. And I didn't smoke, not for a whole year. With my stash right there. That certainly shows I'm no addict. Well, I'm smoking it now again and Debby got up-tight about it at Christmas."

I didn't confess to her that it worried me, too. If I told her I worried, she would then just lie to me in order to keep me untroubled. And I didn't want that. And I had to admit to myself that the only reason I worried was because I didn't know much about it. Alcohol I knew about. I hated and feared its possibilities. It was a known quantity. But pot was another generation, another problem, an unknown.

"Do you smoke a lot?" I said tentatively.

"Not a lot, no. But every day. In the evening. After work."

"With friends? Or alone?" I didn't know what difference it made, but I was edging around the subject gingerly.

"It doesn't matter. Either way. But I'll tell you one thing that's wonderful." A lovely smile of pure pleasure spread over her face. "It's to be reading, alone, and smoke. It's marvelous, fantastic, it opens up all your senses to the book in front of you. You devour it. It comes into you. You mingle with it. I never knew quite how miraculous *Anna Karenina* was until I reread it last month, night after night, with a joint. Daddy always said it was his favorite novel. I know. It goes into my bones and my blood when I read it half stoned. And Proust—oh, my God, Mother, you have no idea about Proust this way. He's so limpid, so lucid, each sensation, each perception shimmering in the light. Not that awful Scott-Moncrieff translation, but the real Proust, simple and mind-piercing as a Bach fugue. I tell you, Proust in the French, with a good stick of hash, it is heaven on earth."

It was almost midnight when we left the restaurant, and we decided to stroll up the Boulevard du Montparnasse for a coffee. The Coupole was closed—August again!—so we went to the corner to the Dôme. We sat on the glassed-in terrace and watched the crowds outside.

"Everyone in London now wears those long Indian cotton skirts. Not so here," I said. "Paris always has its own look, doesn't it?"

"It's all rubbish when they say one place is like another. It just isn't so, I agree. You can always tell you're in Paris."

I stirred the sugar in my tiny *demi* of coffee. "I'd like to buy something for myself here. I haven't really felt like a thing since Daddy died. I did get that skirt and shirt in London, but maybe I'll get some things here, too."

"Oh, you must. And there's a great thrift shop on Edgar Quinet. I'll tell you where. You must go tomorrow." She stuck her feet out to show off her shoes. Tonight, instead of the black leather clogs, she was wearing bright blue suede wedged sandals that matched her blue stockings. "Aren't these great? I got them there. Half price."

"Chippie shoes," I said mockingly.

"I love them. Straight out of the forties." She kept her feet extended, admiring the shoes. The waiter brushed past, making a low remark. She tucked them back under the table. "Old lecher," she said untroubled, "the better to kick him with."

Outside the window of the terrace, we watched the never-ending promenade. A young man spread his wares out on the sidewalk directly in front. First the brown flannel cloth, then, on top of it, handling each piece carefully, he spread out the necklaces and earrings and bracelets of silver, copper, and brass that were precisely like all the others on their flannel cloths, up and down the street. People passed him indifferently, but as he sat back on the curb, cross-legged in front of his little spread, one or two loiterers stopped. A young woman in purple shorts with high white boots and a T-shirt that said MARYLAND COLLEGE knelt to examine one necklace more closely. Her escort, a young black African in a sheepskin coat, watched and then shook his head as she showed him the piece.

We couldn't hear the conversation, but the gestures were scenic.

"Is there a Maryland College?" I wondered.

"Probably not. The French dream up these crazy T-shirts out of thin air. I saw one the other day that said University of Radcliffe. It stopped me. I had to think it out."

The sale outside fell through, and Maryland College and her sheepskin friend disappeared down the street.

"When Geneviève and I were really broke," Abby said, "we were going to do that, too. Make and sell jewelry. It's kind of fun, don't you think? Out in the open air."

"Oh, Abby," I protested, but shut up my protest. "Anyway, how much can you earn? You can't earn that much."

"The word much is relative. No one said much. Just a few francs to tide you over. That's enough much under certain circumstances."

I was silent, sipping my coffee. Had there been times when she was hungry? When she needed those few francs? When I was counting calories in Connecticut, was she really desperate for a meal?

It hurt me to think of it. When Charles and I had talked about it, he was again firm. "It is what she elected to do. This is the life she has chosen. We have no right to interfere."

Reason was on his side. I had only to remember that when we had sent her a hundred dollars as a gift one time, she had written back enthusiastically, ecstatically, about the beautiful red boots she had bought with the money—just what she wanted, just what she *needed*. We were the most marvelous people in the world, just in the nick of time.

The crowds had thinned out somewhat as we walked back, around the corner to the rue Commandant Réné Mouchotte. We agreed not to meet during the daytime on Monday, so she could work.

"Are you sure you'll be okay?" she asked me anxiously.

"Of course. I want to go up to Belleville, anyway. It will be a good time to do it. Don't think about me. I have things to do."

"Belleville? You'll be surprised. It's all changed. Monique went up not long ago and she said she could hardly recognize it at all. So many new projects—old slums all torn down. She said she felt like crying."

"Why like crying? It was not the gayest time of her life." I remembered the story Abby had told me about her friend Monique—how her mother had embroidered the most beautiful yellow star in the neighborhood for Monique's arm band.

"Just the same," Abby answered, "it was her childhood and she remembers it with affection." She laughed. "I suppose her return must have been splendid in her St. Laurent sable-lined raincoat—but it's still old home to her."

"I want to explore up there for a bit, and there are other things I want to do. Don't worry about me tomorrow. Please."

"Okay, Mum. Just don't go to the Delaunay show at the Jeu de Paume. Promise me. I want to see it with you. Save it, so we can go together. Later, when we get back, after the trip."

"I promise. Here, a cab, take it while I watch you, so I'll know you're fine. I'll get upstairs on my own."

"Okay." She embraced me. "Shall we make it early for dinner?"

"Early?"

"Yes, I want to see Jean at nine."

"Of course." I stood talking to her at the door of the taxi. "I'll get something so we can eat at home. Let's eat in, shall we? It will give me a chance to do some food shopping which I love."

She waved from the taxi as it turned out of sight.

# 4

I slipped into bed eagerly. I was tired. But not sleepy. I read some more of the magazines piled high beside the bed. How to make drapes. Hanging plants. A photograph of the new kind of young French husband, helping his beautiful wife with the dishes. Then, suddenly, I remembered how Philippe, Abby's once husband, had called such domesticity demeaning, it turned a man into a *torchon*—a dishrag. Were the times changing as rapidly here as they seemed to be at home? Or was it just a story, as it so often was with us? Philippe!

"I'll never go to sleep if I think about him," I warned myself. "Put him out of your mind. An act of will. He's out of Abby's life completely now. No need to worry. No need to weep. I don't think she's even frightened of him any more."

Philippe. The French boy. That was the title she had given the painting she did of him, from memory, when she was barely seventeen. She had met him in the Village, in

New York, one summer's evening, when he was on a charter flight from France. She came home that night and pushed open my bedroom door. She knew I was awake. I was always awake until each of my children was in the house.

She came now and sat on the empty twin bed next to mine. Charles slept on a studio couch in his own study on the other side of the hall. Ever since we had been able to afford rooms of our own, we had had them. The twin beds were a reminder of the earlier time, when we couldn't. Even before that, there had been the big box-spring and mattress and the one room.

"Mummy," she said, "oh, Mummy. I've met the man I'm going to marry."

"You have?"

"Please don't laugh. This is serious. When I know something, I know it."

She looked so young. She was so young, so defenseless, yet so unbeaten, untrodden, just beginning. She was wearing a big round Breton sailor hat that swept off her face and made it seem translucent, more luminous, paler. It was one of her nights with no makeup. I loved it that way. Mostly she slapped stuff on recklessly, great gobs of eye color and mascara, rarely any lipstick except her awful colorless fad and whatever other teen-age masquerade moved her that minute. Tonight her face was a pure white moon beneath her chestnut hair and that halo of a hat.

She was very solemn, and in spite of my wish to take it all lightly, I had an instinctive wave of apprehension.

"Take off your hat, and you can smoke a cigarette if you want to. Tell me about it."

"He's French. He's here on a student trip from Paris. He's beautiful. His name is Philippe. Oh, Mummy, I love him."

"French? Yes. A student? But where did you meet him? When?"

She mumbled, trying to evade that question. "Down in the Village. Tonight."

"Where in the Village?" I persisted. "A party?"

"Well, sort of." Then she shrugged and laughed. "Well, if you must know, at the Reggie Bar."

That was the era when teen-agers from all over the city drifted to the Village on Sunday afternoons to listen to the folk singing, the guitar playing, everyone singing together. They came like lemmings from Queens and Brooklyn, from the outer reaches of the Bronx, from New Jersey and the fashionable East Side of Manhattan. They came from public schools, parochial schools, private schools, schools in Harlem, schools in Riverdale, and many, school-age, would never see the inside of a school again. Some of our friends prohibited it for their children (who went anyway). We didn't. It was the way it was then, as the decade of the sixties came roaring in. I had gone down with Abby two or three times and thought it was quite wonderful. But a bar?

"A bar?" I said. "Hmmm. That's illegal. And forbidden by us. You know that."

She was patient and firm with me, lecturing me. "Mummy, I'm talking about something crucial. I'm talking about the rest of my life. Not about silly rules."

I had to listen. In spite of myself, I had to recognize the gravity of what she was saying. There was something in the tone of her voice, the set of her chin. "How long will he be in America?" I asked, seeking facts, probabilities.

"He leaves tomorrow. From Newark Airport." She looked at me solemnly. "And I'm going out there to see him off."

No request for permission. A clear statement of intent.

But tomorrow? I felt a sense of reprieve. Tomorrow would certainly cut it short.

Abby came home from Newark, exhausted but triumphant, and went to her room immediately. The painting that emerged three days later was a statement, a pronouncement, a talisman. Against a brilliant cobalt-blue background she had outlined in broad black strokes a young man out of a young girl's dream, poetic, vital, romantic, virile. A shock of yellow hair, electric-blue eyes more vivid than the blue of the background, cigarette dangling from his lips, shirt open to the waist, the whole impulsive and agitated. On the back of the canvas she had brushed the title "The French Boy."

Abby and the French boy were married a year later. They were married in the *mairie* of the Fifth Arrondissement, facing the Panthéon. Charles and I were in Vence, in the South of France, at that time, and Abby had been left to stay in Paris to study at the Grande Chaumière and to take some work at the Sorbonne. We thought we had her well ensconced, protected.

We could have prevented the marriage right then, because Abby was too young by French law to marry without patriarchal permission. But Charles, after a long, tense quarrel between us, gave permission at last. He succumbed, he said, because she was indeed eighteen, the legal age in New York if not in France—but it was simply useful to him as a reason, because, at last, he was relieved that she was being married at all.

At first he had been completely obstinate. He felt that Philippe was marrying her for suspect reasons: to get out of the Army, still fighting in Algeria; to be able to go to the United States to live and work; because Abby was on an allowance, which Charles threatened to cut off if and when the marriage took place. He was frantic with worry and unease.

But Philippe and Abby were already living together, which was not, at that time, as common an arrangement as it is today. Philippe had moved into Abby's little studio and there he was. Charles was wild with frustration, with anger. If we had been able to accept the situation, allowed them to come visit us in Vence, taken it with more equilibrium, there would never have been a marriage at all. By the end of the decade, parents were not only accepting the new moralities, young people themselves were scornful of setting up legal ties. But since this was then—they were married.

Abby wore a lovely white and gold-lamé wedding dress which had been made up overnight. We had put off coming to Paris, hoping to put everything off, but we drove up on a beautiful fall day, a golden autumn day with the sun sifting through the leaves onto the road following the Loire. I rushed Abby at once to a shop on the Rue de Castiglione, where we were able to work out a marvel of a dress designed to conceal the curve of her back, reveal her tiny waist, and be just what she wanted: a little, mini-skirted sugarplum wedding dress that was miraculously finished in one day. We found gold shoes to match, a little gold bag, pale stockings, and somehow, in that same day, between fittings, such other things as nightgowns and leather handbags.

But she was in tears at lunch that day. "I thought you'd never get up here, Mother. Why did you put it off until the very last minute? I thought you'd want to see to all the preparations. You did with Debby."

I couldn't answer her. I had no answer. I had only guilt.

Her question had plagued me in the night for years and

years, as it was doing now, once again, in the heat of Marie-Claude's apartment. It was Charles's obstinacy that had kept me pinned down with him in Vence. I didn't accept his objections to the marriages. They were not mine. But I didn't want to fight him. He was worried about his work and money. And he was ill. His long battle against desperate illness had begun that year. I didn't want to quarrel with him. What I wanted to do was use that age-old female trick of bringing him around.

"I should have fought him on it," I thought now. "Why in hell didn't I fight him? I didn't agree with him about any of it. It wouldn't have made him more sick if I had stood up to him. We should have continued Abby's allowance, paid no attention to her living arrangements, allowed it all to evaporate."

I had my own reasons for fearing the marriage—reasons I had not made entirely clear to Charles, reasons that had to do with irresponsible abortion, which I had to help her with at the last minute; and Abby's private reports of Philippe's deep-going, devastating depressions. I thought that Charles would really blow up, if I told him the truth, and do something silly, like chasing up to Paris with a horsewhip. I thought, better marriage and keeping Abby close to us than a breach that would put her beyond reach. So in some curious kind of tortured convolution, I became the devious champion of the marriage and hung on, hoping to turn Charles around.

He suddenly agreed, seemed relieved by the idea that the situation was being "regularized," and there it was. We drove up just one day before the time Abby and Philippe had set; they were married, and as she and Philippe came tripping down the curving stair of the *mairie*, Philippe's mother offered the most rememberable banality: "There they go, on the road to life."

We had a luncheon party in the private dining room of a Chinese restaurant facing the Sorbonne, a meeting place for Abby and her friends. The food was magnificent, special dishes selected by Abby and Philippe—I remember a spectacular stuffed fish on a yard-long platter—and there was a lot to drink. There were about thirty of us—mostly young people, but Philippe's parents and some of their friends. A young man came in late, greeted with excitement by everyone. He was just home from Algeria.

"What do you do in the Army?" I remember Charles asked him.

"The minimum," he replied.

That called for a toast. This was the very day Kennedy had announced his eyeball-to-eyeball intentions in the missile crisis, and a toast was drunk to everyone's eyeballs. Toasts were drunk to us and we to them. It was all very gay, as if everyone had wanted this. Charles got drunk, and Abby said later that he had embarrassed her. I thought he was fine that night, because I had seen him worse, but she thought it was most unseemly in front of Monsieur and Madame.

"Abby, I can't believe you really mean that," I remember remonstrating with her a few days after the wedding, when she and Philippe were at last with us in Vence. "I haven't the slightest idea what picture you meant us to present to Philippe's parents. We're hardly rich, middle-class, socially proper Americans—nor are we petit-bourgeois French."

Abby flushed. "It's just that Daddy told a dirty joke," she admitted.

"Christ, Abby, so did everyone else."

Her face was red to the hairline. "It's just I didn't want him to do it. He got so drunk."

The four of us loved it in Vence. We wandered around the town together. We cooked and shopped, chatted and sang, and told some truths, some lies. I bought Abby more clothes and we went looking for household goods, leaving Charles and Philippe at their favorite bar.

"What do you need?" I asked as we wandered around the square, stopping at this window and that.

"I'd like a spinning wheel," she said promptly; it had been on her mind. "A spinning wheel like the one in the antique shop on the corner."

I looked at her in disbelief. She didn't have a pot to cook in yet. "A spinning wheel?"

She wore her hair drawn tightly back from her face at this time, in a long pony tail in back. She had a proud young arrogance as she eyed me with disdain. "Yes," she said sharply.

"But that spinning wheel would cost a packet."

"Well, you asked me and that's what I want." I could see her tighten in anger.

"I think it's too expensive," I said flatly. "And you need other things more."

"It may be too expensive, but I know what I want and need." I could have kicked her for the tone of her voice, but it was too absurd. And then I started to laugh. It was just like Abby to want to start housekeeping with an antique spinning wheel. I laughed and laughed, and at first she drew her arm out of mine indignantly and then she began to laugh too. We were weak with laughter when we finally picked up Charles and Philippe and decided to let the household shopping go.

The spinning wheel; I laughed as I thought of it now.

And I had finally found her a spinning wheel up in the Berkshires that went into a corner of her studio in Brooklyn Heights. I stopped my laughter. That poor spinning wheel, I thought. Abby had loved it. It was so nutty.

Charles's illness took us back to the United States very shortly thereafter, leaving Abby and Philippe behind. Soon after, Philippe was drafted but was found psychologically unfit. Abby wrote that the psychological unfitness had been faked to avoid Algeria. She wrote that she went constantly to the army mental hospital to see him, and I was deeply troubled by her faithful visits to the hospital, a long trip from Paris, and the derangement of her life. Then he was released and all seemed well. We didn't see them for almost two years, but we had wonderful letters; they were having fun, going everywhere, Abby was painting, Philippe was teaching, they were living on the sixth floor in a maid's room in the Sixteenth, but Abby had a studio elsewhere and it was perfect.

Then they came for a visit on a charter flight. We were in a country house in the Berkshires and they stayed with us, making trips back and forth to New York. One night, after dinner and on the spur of the moment, they decided not to return to France.

"It will be easier here for us," Abby announced. "All Philippe needs is a green card and he can work. There are all kinds of schools in New York that need French teachers. And I'll go back to the League."

She was pale and thin and I was glad she was going to stay. I told her so.

"Could you help Philippe find a job?" she asked me.

"I'll try. I don't know what I can do, but I'll try."

I did try. I established some non-existing credentials for

him and arranged an interview that won him an excellent spot as teacher at one of the top preparatory schools for boys in the East. It was a superb break for him, a dreadful mistake for her. Returning to life in America meant New York for Abby. It did not mean isolation in the heart of a stylish secondary school in the north of Massachusetts.

Not many months later Abby said to me, shaking her head in grief and accusation. "It was all wrong, Mother, the wrong thing to do. I wanted to be back here so I could live in New York City. What in hell am I supposed to do up there in that frightful place, pour tea?"

"But," I protested. "You asked me to help him."

"Yes, but for a place in New York. Any old kind of place. A yeshiva. A whore house. The Berlitz. Not in a place where we go to dinner every night with a bunch of boys who all stare down my bosom. Some are older than I am, do you know that? And we're supposed to be the master and madam at that lousy table every single night. And the other wives! My God. They all know exactly what to do about everything. They're so *nice*. They wear the same gold circle pin and the same string of pearls and the same Shetland sweaters and they're perfectly all right, but I'm going out of my skin."

I had been wrong, very wrong. But there was no way to undo it. I hadn't counted on Philippe's innate concern for success. Philippe was set on a career and he loved it. It was unexpected affluence and respectability to him. He hadn't been prepared for it, either in fact or in mind. It was the accidental lollipop he had always craved.

Eventually Abby found it intolerable. They made an agreement. He was to stay at the school while she found an apartment in New York, trying to support herself by getting some commercial illustration assignments. Philippe was now entrenched in his school-paid house and resplendent in his little English sports car. He told her that if she worked in New York she could expect no help from him. If she insisted, he might try to get a place in a school in New York. But it would have to be on a par in prestige and salary with the one he was in. He was a tremendous success as a teacher and would now need no intervention from me to help him find another place.

Abby found it very difficult in New York at first. She took a number of odd jobs, too proud to ask us for money and apologetic because Philippe offered none. We used to laugh uneasily about Philippe and money. But it wasn't funny. Every penny he earned was his. So was every penny she was to earn later on.

I breakfasted with her one morning when I came into town, and I remember her shaking her head with tears in her eyes. "I never planned it this way. I never meant it to be like this."

She was barely twenty years old, and her face was as bewildered and forlorn as a child's. She felt defenseless, unarmed. We talked about it. I suggested she forge some economic weapons.

"Get a good portfolio together and make some rounds," I suggested. "These odd jobs are silly. Come up to the Berkshires. There's plenty of place to work. Do some drawings aimed at specific illustrative work."

She did. She completed a portfolio, made the rounds. I still had connections in the city and I gave her names. Almost immediately, assignments came her way. She found a good working apartment in Brooklyn Heights and there followed almost five years of great success. She turned out hundreds of drawings, full-color spreads in fashionable magazines, record covers, book jackets, decorative backdrops for famous Fifth Avenue windows. She began making a lot of money.

By this time Philippe had left the school in the country, had found a place in an equally prestigious private one in the city, and they were back together again in a larger apartment in Brooklyn Heights. They seemed happy, lucky, charming. They went to Europe in the summer; I remember a card from Venice: "We're having a gorgeous time." And we saw them often, sometimes with difficulty, sometimes with tension. Our own problems had magnified. For us they were not good years.

Then things changed—quickly, abruptly. There was a sudden chill. She avoided us. They no longer came to visit. We were now down in Connecticut, only one hour from New York, but the distance between us was strangely widened.

I would call her self-consciously, my voice filled with false cheer and friendliness. She was evasive about dinner, about meeting me in town for the ballet, about coming out. We were upset and worried, wondering how we had offended and cut her off.

The first intimation of the trouble came one afternoon. Philippe telephoned and he was very strange.

"*Allo, allo,*" he called into the phone, his voice gay and high-pitched, "it's Philippe."

"Philippe, yes," I answered, "how good to hear your voice!" But I wondered, as I said this, what he was doing telephoning during school hours.

"I want to sing to you," he said, and he sang. He sang and he rambled, quoted religion, philosophy. He wasn't belligerent or mean. No, rather touchingly affectionate. There was no sequence to what he was saying, yet he kept demanding affirmation, understanding.

"You agree, don't you? You agree," he shouted into the telephone.

He was on the telephone for almost an hour, and I was transfixed as I clung to the desk, and bewildered. I hung up puzzled.

That evening there was another call, and Charles took it. I saw him clutch the telephone tightly, listening, rigid and quiet. That call, too, lasted almost an hour. When Charles hung up he said, "He's crazy."

"Maybe he's been drinking." I tried to push back the thought of madness. "That's what I thought this afternoon."

"He called then, did he? Today?"

"Yes," I admitted. "I thought he was spaced out, drugs."

Charles shook his head. "No. I think it's more serious than that."

There followed almost two months of these telephone calls. We tried to talk to Abby. I called her and told her we had had some weird calls from Philippe.

"Weird?" she said, with a rising inflection, her voice quite challenging and icy, "what do you mean 'weird'?"

"Just weird, Abby." I didn't want to alarm her or close the discussion. I wanted her on that telephone, in the hope that somehow we could be of help. "Maybe he's been drinking too much. Maybe that's it."

"There's nothing weird about Philippe, Mother"; her tone was flat; "and he hasn't been drinking too much. I have no idea what you're talking about."

I didn't pursue it. "When can I see you? It's been a long time."

A long pause. "I don't know. Soon. I'm very busy. I'm working like a dog. Day and night."

"Yes, I know. I see your work around everywhere."

"I'll call you when I'm free."

"Okay, Abby dear. Whenever you're free."

One night, I invited her to join me at the ballet. She accepted and we agreed to meet for dinner at the Russian Tea Room. I was there first and let the waiter put me at a table. There I sat for two hours, waiting, while he glared at me and I nursed a drink and a bottomless anxiety. She finally arrived, pale and reserved, with only the vaguest apology for being so late.

"I worried about you," I said, trying not to show anger or concern. "I called your house to see if you had forgotten."

She stiffened in rage. "You called the apartment? Why did you do that?"

I thought, what an idiot question! Of course I called her apartment. I had been sitting here for two hours. I blinked at her in wonderment.

"Who answered?" she asked, shaking as she lit a cigarette.

"No one, Abby. There was no answer." Again I did not press it. There was something here that could not be pressed, could not be probed. I was frightened.

The crack in the ice came soon. The telephone rang in Westport one night. As I flipped on the light to answer it, I saw it was after two in the morning.

"Mummy!" It was Abby's voice, a child's voice, shaking in panic over the telephone. "Come at once. Oh, my God. Come at once."

"Of course I'll come. Of course."

Charles had heard the telephone ring down below and was on the extension.

"Go get ready," he said to me on the phone, then spoke to Abby: "What is it? Tell me while your mother gets ready. Of course she'll come."

"He's gone crazy. He's trying to kill me. He's slashed all my paintings. Broken the furniture. Oh, Daddy, I don't know what to do."

"Do? Only one thing. Listen to me carefully. Get out of the apartment at once. Is there someone you know near by?"

"Yes. Leslie and Dick."

"Good. Go over there."

"It's so late."

I could hear him answer as I ran downstairs, "It doesn't matter that it's late. Go there. At once. What's the address?" He turned to me: "Atlantic near Clinton, okay. I've just told your mother. Stay there. She'll be there quickly, she'll pick you up."

"What about Philippe?" she wailed on the telephone. "What about him? He might hurt himself. Oh, Daddy."

"Don't worry. Go, this instant. I'll call the police in Brooklyn from here. They'll help him. They'll get him to a hospital. Now. Run."

I stood there beside him as he hung up the telephone. I had managed slacks and sweater, no socks, my hair undone under a scarf. We embraced.

"Drive carefully," he said, then added bitterly, "I'm a fucking cripple. This is my job. But, god-damn it, all I can do is make the phone calls."

I held him close for an instant. He pushed me toward the door. "Hurry, hurry." His face was shrunken with pain. I reached into his room for his cane, which he had forgotten in the rush to answer the dread night ring of the telephone.

"Take it easy, darling," I said as I kissed him again. "Get off your feet. I'll let you know when I get there."

I found Abby at her friends' apartment, huddled in a chair, shivering like a waif, in a little cotton house dress that seemed like a costume for bedlam. Was this her own snake-pit uniform? Was madness catching?

We went back to her apartment together. Police were in front of it, Philippe leaping and jumping on the roof. The police talked him down. He saw us standing in the crowd in front of the stoop. "Come along for the ride," he shouted gaily at us, "let's make a night of it."

"Mother, Mother." Abby clutched me closely. "We can't let him go by himself. We've got to go along. He needs us."

We identified ourselves to the police and rode in one of the cars to Long Island Hospital, around the corner. There, after an hour, it was decided to send him to Kings County Hospital, and we went with him. The police insisted that he be admitted there for examination. We all waited together—Philippe, the police, Abby, and I—in the Kings County reception room; and while we waited, Philippe paced up and down, talking endlessly, laughing, warning Abby that if they kept him, it would be her fault and she should be sure to bring him cigarettes and oranges the very next day.

Finally, Philippe was taken to another room, followed by the policeman, who emerged a few minutes later to say that he was being admitted and we should go.

"Oh, my poor Philippe, my poor Philippe, what will they do?" Abby stood wringing her hands pathetically and crying. I put my arms around her shoulders and led her into the gray beginnings of the new day.

"Oh, Mother, what will happen?"

It was almost five o'clock in the morning. I hoped that

what would happen would be that that particular part of the leaden Brooklyn sky would fall on that particular corner of the hospital that housed Philippe and knock him dead.

But the sky never falls. Philippe was in the psychiatric ward for almost three months, and during all that time Abby stayed at the Brooklyn Heights home of friends of ours, who nurtured her and cared for her and tried to get her out of that front-porch cotton dress and back to concern for herself. She went every day to the hospital with oranges, cigarettes, cake. I came to Brooklyn to be with her, as often as I could. I helped her clean up the horrible mess in the apartment, the slashed pictures, the shattered furniture, the spinning wheel in splinters, the broken glass everywhere. I visited Philippe with her, talked to him, tried to reassure him, urged him to think of going back to France and the arms of his mother. Because Philippe asked me to, I even called the headmaster of his school to try to hold his job for him, describing this episode as a nervous breakdown.

My only true concern was Abby. One afternoon, as we sat in the big, barren reception room of Kings County, waiting for our separate passes to go up to visit him, she told me of the fright and turmoil of the previous two years. Philippe's manic behavior had begun with money.

"There's something sick about Philippe and money, Mummy; you must have known that a long time ago," she said to me quietly.

We were sitting on a long wooden bench, an old black man beside me with a brown paper bag that he kept rustling and opening and poking his hand into constantly to verify the contents. On Abby's side, a little woman, Abby's size, with pinched sad face, clinked her charm bracelets and tried to listen to us. Abby lifted her shoulder to keep her out while we talked.

"I made so much money the last few years, you wouldn't believe it."

I would. I was quite aware of the rich rewards for successful advertising illustration.

"I was pinned down to the drawing board. I became a machine. That's why I couldn't see you. Couldn't face you and Daddy. You didn't approve of Philippe, anyway." I tried to protest, but she pushed this aside impatiently. "No, you never did. It hurt me, but you never did. But all that money, it drove Philippe crazy, it was three or four times what he was making—so he blew it all. He'd go into a bar and buy drinks for everyone in the place, anything they wanted. He bought out all the bookstores on Montague Street and in New York, first editions, fine bindings. They're still there in the apartment. You saw them when we tried to clean up. Wherever he could, he spent my money." Now her voice turned bitter. "His own, of course, goes carefully into a bank in France, managed by Mama; he intends to buy property there." She began to cry.

"He says I'm a real painter, a genius, but he doesn't want me to waste time painting; he wants a money machine, not a painter. Oh, Mummy, how evil, how cruel; he slashed my paintings; sick, sick, sick." She was sobbing bitterly, and the young woman next to her leaned over and put her arm around her shoulder.

"No cry, little girl, no cry," she said. "*Muy triste. La vida muy triste.*"

Abby managed a wan smile. "*Gracias,*" she said, "*gracias.*"

Yes, life was sad and the sadness lasted longer than it should have, but it passed. The psychiatrists at the hospital loaded her down with responsibility and guilt. They insisted that her place was with Philippe, that she must sustain him. They told her that if she did not provide a place for him to come home to, he could not be released. One young doctor called me in Westport and asked me to meet him in a restaurant near the hospital to talk. I agreed. He was about thirty years old, and he sat there telling me that my daughter "owed" it to Philippe to see him through.

"Why does she *owe* it to him?" I tried to speak to him calmly but I was enraged. The narrow-minded psychiatric attitude that concerned itself only with the patient appalled me. "My daughter is twenty-four years old. Do you think her life is less valuable than his?"

He hadn't thought about it that way, he said. It was just that Philippe had to have a home to go to or he could not be released.

We had Abby talk to a doctor on the outside, who told her to run, get out, as fast as she could. Philippe was not her problem, the doctor said. "You must protect yourself," he told her. "If you don't, you should examine the reason why. You are your responsibility. No one else."

Abby managed to do it both ways. She did accept Philippe as her problem, her responsibility, in order to get him released, to find him a place to come home to, to sustain him until he went back to teaching in another school. When that was done, she moved out of Brooklyn into New York and away.

But the fear did not disappear, not for a very long time. Philippe did not permit it. She never knew when he would ring her doorbell. Even after her return to Paris to live, he came ringing her bell, taunting her with her poverty while he grew fatter and more secure. Real estate in France, real estate in Brooklyn. One day when he rang her bell and she descended, she found him with a young woman on his arm. His mistress, he bragged. They went to have coffee together.

"See," said Philippe, pointing to the young woman's new coat, "St. Laurent. I bought it for her. I see you're wearing the same old number."

She told me about this on one visit, and when I started to laugh, although I was furious, she laughed too. "He really is a bastard," she said, quite happy about it. "You know the bastard even refused to pay two hundred dollars towards our divorce, although he's the one who wanted it; his beauty queen insisted. What a pompous ass he is now; good riddance."

The French boy. When I thought of the way Abby looked now in Paris, so staunch, so vibrant, at the top of her powers, painting surely, slowly, confidently; in love, loved in return, surrounded by friends; I ached at the unhappiness of those other years. It had robbed her of part of her twenties. No matter that when she talked of Philippe now, it was without anger, even a kind of pleasant contempt. No matter that Debby had once said, "They were destructive to one another, Mother. Abby is determined about her work. That's the thing. Everything else is secondary." No matter any of it —it had been a loss of time, deep-going wounds too soon. I twisted and turned in the endless, sleepless night in my own rage at those sad years.

# 5

Morning came at last and I awakened to a bright, sunny day. I had fallen asleep somewhere in the dark past and now it was Monday. There were many things I wanted to do. Arrange the car rental for Wednesday morning; go to Abby's place about noon to pick up my luggage and finally get it set for the month's stay; pick up my camera bag, too, for I wanted to walk around the Fifteenth Arrondissement and take some pictures.

"I'll go to Belleville tomorrow," I decided. It seemed too hot, even now, at nine o'clock, for that long subway ride to the distant north of town. And I loved the Fifteenth. It was always fun to roam around the Champs de Mars, the Rue du Commerce, the Avenue de la Motte-Picquet, the Place Breteuil. These were places out of my own Paris history, when I had been young and a sometime part-time baby sitter, parading my charges in the lush green parks of left-bank elegance.

I ground the coffee beans, as I had at last learned to do, on the little machine in the kitchen, and made a large potful. I even heated some milk, feeling very at home, as I sipped three full cups of coffee and milk instead of my usual black brew. I nibbled my way through some *biscottes*. I felt luxurious and replete.

Then a hot bath with Marie-Claude's tantalizing bath salts. I found an iron and ironing board and pressed the black cotton slacks and the black tunic. I felt good in this place all to myself in Paris. For the hundredth time, I felt a wave of gratitude to Abby for thinking of it and arranging for it.

"How perceptive!" I thought, "how canny of her to know and understand what would heal me now." I had been reluctant to come, I had thought I needed a dark corner somewhere to hide in; but this was a light spot, it was wonderful, really, it served me well. I put out of mind the megrims that descended on me without warning.

I stretched lazily, looking out the window. The same buses in front of the Paris-Sheraton, exactly the same crowd filing into the hotel.

"Must be a film," I thought, "they keep running it over and over again." I felt a flash of superiority because I wasn't stuck in a hotel. I finished getting dressed and chattered to myself, "I'm not in a hurry. I'll walk to Abby's. I'll pick up some food. Then come right back here with my cameras and suitcase. I'll get out of her way at once, for the day."

I descended the long, broad staircase that led from the outside apartment ramp down to the street and turned left. I had noticed a Europecar rental office in the garage at the corner and decided to get that errand out of the way first.

In a corner of the garage, in a kind of little boxed booth, was the office. The young man in charge filled out the forms and took my reservations for a Simca, with all the paper-work and pomposity that might have gone into the purchase of a château.

"It's cheaper by the week," he whispered conspiratorially, "unlimited mileage."

"Fine," as I counted the days in my mind, Wednesday, Thursday, Friday, Saturday, maybe Sunday and Monday. Did that make a week?

The young man and I carefully considered the calendar.

"Of course," he said, poking his pencil at each of the days under discussion, "exactly."

"Suppose we want to come home sooner?" I asked. I did want to be flexible. Abby had work to do. I didn't want her to become restless if she changed her mind. "And it's best to be flexible, isn't it?"

"Don't worry," the clerk assured me with a grand gesture, "we'll just make it for the other rate. Whichever comes out best for you, we'll do."

It sounded splendid and I went off, promising to pick up the car at nine-thirty on Wednesday morning.

I found Abby eager and happy to see me. "What hap-pened? I thought you'd be here for breakfast." I noticed that my bags had reappeared from under the bed where Abby had hidden them and were ready and waiting to go.

"Ha!" I said as I hugged her. "Can't wait to get rid of my luggage."

She blushed and hugged me back. "Oh, Mummy," she agreed, "you know how I am. I hate anything out of place. But you do need your stuff and we'll grab a cab and get it all over to the apartment right away, after we eat."

We sat on her little balcony and nibbled the croissants

she had bought that morning, drank some tea and cut into some apples and cheese. The garden below was greener than it had been.

"They watered," she said in a hushed, furtive tone. "The authorities have cautioned against it, but they watered anyway. I'm so glad." We chuckled. "Such a beautiful unmentionable, isn't it?" she said. "I just adore being here."

"I wish, in a way," I said, "that my own garden was below a balcony and someone else had to weed and plant and water."

"It's the best kind," she agreed. The thought of the garden in Connecticut swept over us both that moment. We looked at each other quietly. I put my hand on hers.

"The rock you painted weathered the winter marvelously. I'm so glad it's there."

"I'm glad too," she said, her eyes filling with tears. "I'm so glad. I wanted to ask. I wasn't entirely sure of that acrylic paint."

"It's just as you left it. I can see it every time I look out the bedroom window. Even when it was covered with snow, I knew it was there."

She sounded anxious. "If it needs fixing or retouching, I'll do it when I come back next time."

"It's really fine."

"Dear *Daddy.*" She shook her head, then put her sleeve up to wipe her eyes. "Dear, dear *Daddo.* I'll never get over him, Mummy, never."

"Neither will I. Never." I put my hand over hers again, across the little table. "But wouldn't he have loved our garden party and that stone? Wouldn't he have loved it!"

We broke into laughter. "And wasn't Debby a riot with her glass of wine?"

Our funeral picnic, we called it, with me and Debby and Abby to do the final honors, the last fling for Charles. The postdeath procedure had taken a week and John could not stay until the end because of his work in California.

"Don't worry about that, darling," I had reassured him. "We're not going to do anything. Certainly no memorial service or any such stuff. You've been wonderful. You and Patti have jobs. There's no need to hang around."

Indeed, he had been wonderful. Taking over all the arrangements after the post-mortem, going through the grim business of release from the morgue to the undertaker, and then signing the papers for cremation. He had spared me the telephone calls and the decisions. Charles's death, from spinal meningitis, was complicated by the long-standing aplastic anemia. The doctors asked for an autopsy for research purposes. (One young doctor was so eager that he asked even before Charles's death, to my horror.) I agreed. The delay until Friday was thus a technicality. There was no reason for John to stay. We had all had seven long days with a constant stream of friends and family for breakfast, lunch, and dinner. Food had appeared from all sides; casseroles and lasagne and cheese and cakes and things to drink. We had been warmed and sustained by love and concern. But we were all tired. I was ready to fall, nervous and jittery. When it was all over with, it would at least be over with.

Now at last the undertaker telephoned, the ashes would be delivered on Friday at eleven-thirty in the morning. Debby put up a sign on the front door: PLEASE DO NOT DISTURB. WE'RE ALL WELL. AND WE'LL BE BACK WITH THE DOOR OPEN AFTER 2:00 O'CLOCK.

Before his departure, John had carried into the house a

rock that Abby had chosen on the hillside beyond our house. They had gone out together to look for it and he carried it back, setting it on the newspapers spread over the dining-room table, where she wanted it. Then she had gone over to the art store in town and bought some acrylic paint.

We all watched her as she got ready to paint.

"What shall we put on the rock, Mother? What do you want on it?" they all asked.

I didn't have to think at all. I knew. "Love you . . . always did," I said.

Abby flushed. That was "her say." Those were her words.

When she had been a little girl, sent to camp for the first time, her initial letter arrived: "Please send my underpants—love you, always did." That "love you . . . always did" became a code between Charles and me of the greatest endearment, the deepest affection, the words that linked us with one another and with our children. We always signed our letters to one another that way. We said it to one another in good times and bad.

"Love you . . . always did," repeated Abby, and she dipped her brush into one of the bottles and rolled it clean on the paper, her hand steady.

"Then his initials," said Debby. "The way he always had them on those Brooks Brothers shirts of his."

The rock was still on the dining-room table, decorated with flowers and hearts, a gay, glad valentine in blues and whites and pinks and reds—"love you, c.o.g., always did"—when the tin with the ashes arrived.

Debby carried the tin, in a shining box like a brand of cheap tobacco, out to the rose garden, near the sundial. Then the three of us hauled the rock out to the back. Abby was jumpy, skittery. "Don't drop it. Oh, it's not good enough. I made the lettering too big."

We put the rock down in place before the sundial.

"Would Daddy like it?" Abby cried, shaking with her uncertainty. "Do you think he'd like it? Is the lettering too big?"

Debby and I embraced Abby, circling her, trying to reassure her. "It's beautiful, it's beautiful," we told her. "He'd love it."

Debby brought out a picnic basket and a bottle of wine. We sat cross-legged on the grass while Debby dug a hole to put the box in, and we set it down carefully into the hole but not yet covering it. Then Debby read a poem by Christopher Levenson and I read *Dover Beach,* and then we opened the lunch basket and the wine and had a lovely picnic.

By the end of the bottle, it was time to cover the ashes and be done. We all felt the alcohol and the sun and the excitement a bit, and suddenly Debby, pink with the wine, leaned over with her glass above the box in the ground and said, "I'd love to have Daddy have a sip, just one last sip for luck."

Abby pulled back Debby's hand abruptly before she could tip the glass.

"Debby, don't do that," she cried out severely. "He worked so hard to stay sober."

This was so funny, the three of us broke into wild laughter. Then Debby filled the earth back into the hole and we sang "The Worker's Flag Is Deepest Red" and "Roll Over, Mabel," and went back into the house.

As we sat now in the warm sun on the balcony, Abby said softly, "How bright and sunny and gay it was that day, we

were so all together, John and Patti too, we were all together."

We finished our lunch and I helped her carry the cups
and dishes into the kitchen.

"I'll wash them," I said.

"No, no. Let them be, Mother. Let's get your luggage out
and settled. Come on."

She insisted on hauling my bag down the flight of stairs to
the entrance of the building.

"Please let me." I tried to take over.

"Come on, you shouldn't," she said. "I'll run around the
corner to the taxi stand on Alésia. You stay here."

I saw her fly down the street toward the big blank area
where the park would one day be. She literally flew, lifting
herself high as a dancer, the full skirt of that black dress
catching the breeze, her blue legs like wings. She seemed to
move like a bird, above the cobbled street and the rutted
sidewalk; then she was lost from sight around the corner.

"Those exercises," I thought; "what a miracle they've
been!" She hadn't mentioned any pain during these last few
days. Was it to spare me? In the past, the pain had been
unrelenting. Her back throbbed when she stood at the easel
or bent over the drawing board. Once, one of the doctors
had asked her what she did, how she worked. When she explained, he said briskly, "Give it up, your back can't take it."

She gave him up instead and learned some helpful tricks
at the clinic. How to lie on the floor, flat against the hard
wood, to rest; how to carry heavy packages or a heavy bag
with her right arm, or to avoid them altogether (except
mine, I thought; what a drag!); how to hang from a bar
over the door. But with it all, had the pain completely disappeared?

It was hard to tell. She seemed so gay, so full of laughter, so light on her feet. The occasional wince, the drawn look, came always as a shock and a reminder to me. Or perhaps it was the other way around. The wince and the drawn look tightened my chest with the pain and concern that was constant in me, too.

A taxi rounded the corner from the Rue Bardinet and she leaped out of it. She lifted my bag (again I remonstrated) and tossed it into the luggage rack the driver had opened. I kept my camera bag and we got in.

"But, Abby, love, you don't have to come with me now. I'll manage all of this up to the apartment myself."

"No. It won't take long. I'll just go up and back. I'd rather see you installed. Anyway, how can you manage this junk yourself?"

"Okay. You're right."

She sighed. "You just take too much. It's a bore." She leaned over in the taxi and smacked my cheek with a deep kiss. "But it's okay. I love you, anyway."

The taxi was admitted through the guarded gate leading up the ramp to the apartment house.

"Could you carry the bag into the lobby?" I asked the driver. He looked surprised. The hell with it. We hauled everything together, up the lobby, into the elevator, and at last at Marie-Claude's.

Abby sighed with relief. "Well, you're settled now. Can I help put things away?" She looked around the apartment vaguely, detached.

"You're eager to get away," I answered. "Why don't you go. I know you want to work."

She nodded and then smiled ruefully. "You don't mind,

Mummy? I have a thing going now and I don't want to interrupt."

"Oh, no, no." I kicked the suitcase. "Thank you for helping. You're an angel. Go now. I'm all set."

She hugged me. "I'll see you later, then. But you do remember, don't you"—she sounded a bit hesitant—"not too late for dinner. I want to see Jean."

I, too, hesitated. "Would you like to skip dinner tonight, darling? It will be all right with me. I'll find something to do."

"Oh, no. Never. Don't be silly. Just let's make it earlier than usual. I'll be here at seven-thirty."

She was out the door then and I could see, as I looked down from the window to the avenue below, that she turned and walked briskly to the Avenue du Maine and the subway. I unpacked my camera, put some new film into the Nikkormat, and decided definitely on the stroll through the Fifteenth that had been on my mind.

I spent all afternoon up and down the Boulevard Pasteur, over to the Military School, the Avenue de Breteuil, still as grand and well-heeled as it had ever been. The memory of my little Dominique and Françoise and Victoire flashed through my mind, and their enormous apartment. Which building? I couldn't remember. I smiled as I remembered how they had teased me because I could never get the word *rouge* right for them. I was supposed to teach them English and take them to the park. They used to dance in front of me repeating over and over, "*Dites rouge, mademoiselle, dites rouge,*" and then scream happily at the sound of my misplaced *r*, my long *u*.

I sat down to rest on one of the benches at the Place Breteuil, enjoying the banality of the circles of red geraniums around the circles of blue ageratum around the circles of gray-green artemisia. So pretty, almost a caricature of what Vita Sackville-West always, and contemptuously, called municipal gardening; but so easy on the eye. It was all so easy on the eye here; how had Dominique and Françoise and Victoire made it with the Germans? I shook the question from my mind and continued on my walk.

There were some shops open, smugly elegant and fantastically expensive-looking: one, completely devoted to down comforters and quilts, had such an air about it of insufferable money that I was tempted to go in and annoy the clerk by asking the prices of things.

Abby adored looking at shops like this. "Aren't they the most vulgar concoctions?" she would chortle. "Aren't they awful? Would you even have one of these things if they gave it to you free?" She would shake her head. "No one does this particular kind of *luxe* like the French; it's so *nouveau ancien régime.*"

I passed an antique shop with a fascinating clutter in the window. Toward the rear of the display was a beautiful black satin evening bag with a giant reddish-pink rose embroidered on it, all mounted on an elaborate engraved silver frame with a thin silver chain.

"Abby would just love that," I thought, struck by it, "Oh, she'd love it. It's just the kind of thing she adores." I became fired by the thought of buying it for her. I went into the tiny shop filled to the brim with those chains and beads and doll's heads and feather fans that tell you the minute you enter, this is a good place. The kind of shop where everything old is terribly new and much in fashion and where the smell is a mix of mode and must.

The proprietor wore purple velvet slacks and a dreamy

pink silk shirt. "The handbag?" he responded to my question. "Superb, isn't it? And madly fashionable. Cheap, really; it's August, you know."

"How much," I interrupted the flow, "how cheap?"

It really was cheap, especially since he pointed out that the frame was real silver.

"Only 150 francs," he said. I calculated, about thirty dollars. It was wonderful. I opened it.

"Impeccable," the proprietor said, "note how impeccable."

It was. Every stitch in place and the embroidered rose was the same red-pink as the single rose that still bloomed below in Abby's garden now.

But, cheap or not for what it was, I hesitated at the thought of thirty dollars. I knew she'd love it. But we were going away. I'd buy it on my return, maybe I could get it for less. It would be my parting gift to her.

"Thank you so much. It pleases me. I'll probably be back." I left the alluring shadows of the little shop to follow again the avenue outside.

But I was annoyed with myself as I walked. "Why didn't I buy it? It's just her kind of thing. I hope it isn't sold until we get back." I nagged myself with my anxiety, with the kind of indecision over trivialities I often suffered. As I walked, I weighed the matter fretfully.

Her little mirrored dressing table, set in a corner of her tiny bathroom, was hung with a variety of enchanting evening bags acquired through the years. The little black velvet embroidered pouch from Pont-Aven that I bought for her when she was thirteen. The hammered silver mesh for her fifteenth birthday. The Art Deco mesh I had found on Route 7 in Connecticut. The paisley pouch she had found herself in a thrift shop on Third Avenue in New York, then had loaned to me for five years, asked for it back two years ago, and had just returned to me yesterday, when I saw it hanging there and lamented its absence from my life.

"You take it now, Mummy. It's your year for it."

I grabbed it eagerly. "Sure?"

"Of course I'm sure. Look"; she gestured at the clutter displayed on the wall; "see all I have."

But this rose-embroidered one—it would send her into raptures. Damn it, why hadn't I bought it? But financial caution prevailed, and although I passed the shop again on my return home, I decided to put off any purchases until Abby and I were back in Paris.

I was tired when I returned to the apartment, but decided to put my camera away and go out again to buy some food for our dinner. It would be pleasant to eat in the apartment, since Abby wanted to leave directly after dinner. I thought of some chicken, so simple to roast, some string beans, sliced tomatoes, some cake. All easier said than done. I hadn't realized it was Monday—a closing day in Paris for most little shops—and finally dragged my way through the supermarket around the corner, the only store open. I came home loaded with shopping bags.

"How great everything smells!" Abby sniffed voluptuously when she arrived. "A home-cooked meal. Marvelous."

"Come in. Let's have a drink first. Here's some of the house vermouth. After all, Marie-Claude did say to help ourselves to anything we found." I poured the vermouth into tumblers, added ice and water. We clicked glasses. "Don't you ever cook at home, love?"

"Oh, yes. But it's Jean who's really the cook. He's a superb cook. He takes the whole thing over, when he's there. I'm just the scullery maid."

She took a long swallow. "He gets me to chop, chop, mince, mince. He's a demanding cook. It's too much. Anyway, cooking just isn't my thing. I love to shop on the Rue Didot for little bits and pieces. But planning a meal, cooking it—ugh—it's a waste of time."

Then she smiled with delight. "Remember that dairy shop on the Rue Didot, Mummy? What a place! fantastic! All that tile work on the ceiling and the walls. All white and blue and mirrored and so *normande*. And the way they stack those eggs. By color, by size, each one so precious. And all those cheeses and Monsieur and Madame. Fabulous, like something out of *The Best Butter*."

"*The Best Butter?*" I questioned her. "But the people in that book were not very nice, were they? Black market and stuff."

"Yes, pigs," said Abby firmly. "Just plain collaborators. But what do you think? Like most of the French."

"Why, Abby!" I was surprised. "I never heard you critical of the French before."

She flushed. It was apparent that she was troubled. "I love my friends," she said. "I really love the friends I have here in France. But, let's face it, collaboration was endemic."

"But you're all a new generation, you and your friends. Hardly even born during the occupation."

Her tone remained firm. "They won't even admit it existed."

I put the dinner on the table and we sat facing one another as she plunged in, in her usual ferocious style, smacking her lips and laughing with pleasure as she repeated how good it all was.

I continued our earlier conversation. "I heard that *The Sorrow and the Pity* was a smash success. Crowds on the

Champs Élysées to see it. Aren't there questions about those days?"

She raised her head from her food, her voice intent. "What do you mean, crowds to see it? It was barely visible. One or two theaters on the Champs Élysées. And only a select group of people went, those who knew about it anyway. Besides, it's a documentary about the Auvergne and the resistance there. That makes it like a fairy tale to most Parisians, a fantasy in a faraway place. And don't forget: it's not about Jews."

That's true. It isn't.

She continued, her voice now quite strained. "I don't understand anything about anything any more, Mother. I really don't. But there is so much anti-Semitism here in France. Among the warmest and most marvelous people."

"Among your friends?" I asked.

She held her knife and fork bolt upright on the table and lowered her head toward them. "Yes," she said, "among my friends, too. It is impossible to deny it. It hurts me. It hurts me deeply. These are people I care about."

I ate quietly for a while and she did too; then she shook her head. "I don't understand the insistence Debby has in making a point of her cultural heritage, as she calls it, with David. Dear God, David is about an eighth Jewish. I'm not on that side, either."

"I guess I'm not, either," I admitted, "but we're in the era of ethnicity," I tried to joke without being critical. I myself felt that one heritage was quite as accidental as another. But ethnic interest was in the wind now.

"Ethnicity!" Abby exploded. "Not in France. And I find it a banal idea. Don't you?"

I shrugged.

"But I detest anti-Semitism," Abby went on. "There is such suspicion here. And they feel so strongly about the Israelis. But there's the other side, too. That noisy bunch of hoodlums with the Star of David on their naked chests, throwing Molotov cocktails. I can understand objecting to that. That's political. That's not anti-Semitism. You can go along with it or oppose it. I'm not concerned with the political. What worries me is the bone-deep, visceral anti-Semitism. Not the anti-Israel," she stressed the point, "but the plain old dirty-Jew feeling." She shuddered. "I hate to think of what could happen in the future."

I felt the chill of her fear. "But you're French now, Abby. What will you do about it?"

"Do about it? Nothing. Stay here. It's only one ugliness, you know. Only one thing, not the whole. And do you think it doesn't exist at home? Even in New York?"

"It's not the same thing at home," I said. It was customary to deny anti-Semitism in America.

"Maybe. If people don't know what you think or what your background is, they feel free to say the things they really mean, and maybe it's not scary at home, but it is there, underneath—no, not even underneath, spoken out, all the time."

"But it never takes power at home."

"It never has, Mother; that's not to say it can't or won't. It did here because it was ripe and ready and it served almost everyone's interest to go along with the occupation. After all, a government is a government. Most people try to manage the best way they can under any regime. Most people are screwed all the time anyway. How many revolt against anything? And they're right. One terror is the same as another."

"Do you really feel that way?"

"Me? I hate the idea of the Nazis. I hate the idea of authority. I hate terror. It frightens me, bone-deep." That hot red flush crept up to her hairline. "All I want to do is paint. I don't want to control anyone. I don't want anyone to control me." She paused; something else was troubling her. Then she went on: "That's part of my feeling about the feminist movement. I know Debby and her ideas about it. I respect her. But I don't always think she's right. I really don't. And sometimes I think she feels I'm a dummy." She looked sad for a moment. "We really don't see eye to eye on it. I don't want a world controlled by women just because they're women."

"Neither does Debby," I said. "She wants a changed world. She's a radical, you know, just as much as she's a feminist."

"What does that mean? It has to be defined. Radical what?"

I picked crumbs off the table carefully. "Radical Marxist, I guess."

"Marxist? Oh? Debby's a Marxist? Well." Again, silence. "Maybe then I won't argue with her any more. I never argue with Marxists. They're too rigid. And I don't want to argue with Debby." Again she sounded sad. "I love her so. I feel terrible when I seem dumb to her."

Abby's uncertainty again, her lack of confidence. It cropped up all the time. So sure of herself in so many ways and then so easily intimidated, engulfed by her feeling that she didn't have the university education we had wanted her to have, and now regretting what had been offered and rejected.

In a year when admission to college had been difficult,

she had been accepted everywhere she applied; but so determined had she been to get to Paris and Philippe, that we
did not know she had been accepted by the Cornell University School of Fine Arts (where we particularly wanted
her to go) until two months after the acceptance had arrived and we found it hidden behind the dining-room buffet,
where she had stuck it. Instead, she had gone off, proud
to be taken as a second-year student, to the Boston Museum
School, where she smoked more pot than she painted, and
insisted, after four months, that she could not bear it.

Why? she had argued with us at that time, since Charles
and I were going to France to live, couldn't she go in advance to Paris to study? We finally allowed it and a promise
was made to her that as long as she was formally involved in
study, we would send her an allowance.

Later this became a bitter bone of contention. "But he
promised," she passionately insisted, angry with her father,
"and I *am* studying. What difference does it make if Philippe
is living in the studio too?"

It was only in the last few years that she voiced any
regret about a college education. She never expressed it
fully, but she had asked Debby and her father and me about
books to read. She had made careful lists; and she read—
carefully, selectively, each chosen book, over and over
again.

I brought the dessert to the table—the little cakes I had
bought that afternoon. She gobbled them without thinking,
one, two, three. Then she looked at me, up through her
thick shadowy black lashes and burst into her peals of
laughter. "I know. I'm a greedy goat." She wiped her fingers
on the paper toweling I had put out as napkins. "But,
Mother," she reopened our conversation, "I never ran into as

much prejudice anywhere as I did at the Dalton School. It's true. If you weren't pure-bred Temple Emanu-El, you weren't quite right. And talk about Spics? There we were, ten blocks from Spanish Harlem, and they acted as if we were defending the Alamo. One time, I picked up a kid on Eighty-sixth Street at the five and ten, a cute Puerto Rican, and he walked me back to the school. You have no idea the things that were said to me, even by the teachers."

I gestured weakly. "You were only fifteen, after all. And Dalton is changed now. I guess they were afraid of the danger."

"Danger!" she exploded. "What danger? He was about fifteen years old himself. Danger, my ass. It was because he was a Puerto Rican, simply that." She wagged her head incredulously. "Anyway, he was the one I painted. Remember that painting? My crazy period. All blacks and blues. Mr. Fogarty loved it. I gave it to Pedro, remember? He came to the house." Again her laughter. "I gave it to him as a present, to take home to hang in his room, the poor thing. He was flabbergasted by it. Maybe his mother threw it out, not knowing it was a masterpiece."

I remembered. I had been annoyed when she had given that painting away so casually. It was a stunning work, painted on a large wild scale, broad brushstrokes, but with the control, the grasp that had begun, even then, to characterize her work.

She chuckled. "Maybe Pedro's mother bawled him out because what was such a nice, good Catholic Puerto Rican boy doing below Ninety-sixth Street, collecting filthy pictures."

We moved from the table to the low couch for our coffee. I noticed the time. Twenty to nine. Nine, she had said, for her date with Jean. I didn't want to keep her, but didn't want to remind her. It was, after all, her affair. And she seemed in no hurry.

Abby loved to talk, I loved to listen. I loved to talk, she always listened with her own special kind of close attention. We ran on and on to one another. She was instinctive and immediate and articulate with words. She had a poetic and precise way of reaching into the heart of an idea and saying the most complex things simply. It made her letters a joy. It colored our conversations with perceptions and sensitivities that were always new and fresh to me.

"Tell me," she asked now, "about this Jimmy Carter. Jimmy! For President! What do you know about him? Are you worried?"

"Worried?" I nodded to her in our common bewilderment. "I don't know anything about him, really. But why worry?"

"*Le Monde* had a long piece on him. They called him a plantation owner from the Deep South. It sounds ominous."

"Oh, Abby," I laughed. "*Le Monde* is too grave about it. He's a successful peanut farmer from Georgia—he was governor once. Did *Le Monde* say he had black peons that he whipped each day?"

"Not exactly." She sounded perturbed. "But does he? After all, those acres and acres of peanuts down there in the South."

"It's just like the French to see it that way. Anyone rich makes it off someone, of course; but he's just a rich farmer, hardly a plantation owner in the Old South. The French and we never get one another straight, do we?"

"But tell me about him, Mother. What does he stand for? What's he all about?"

It was now past nine and I tried to tell her what I knew

about Jimmy Carter and why I probably wouldn't vote for him, although there were lots of reasons why I probably would, and she listened and asked questions and had another cup of coffee and smoked her endless cigarettes until I saw it was past nine-thirty.

"Abby, darling." I pointed to the clock. "I just noticed. It's past nine-thirty. Didn't you have a date?"

She leaped up. "Oh, yes. Oh, Mummy, I hate to go." She hurried, gathering up her crushed package of cigarettes, her little basket handbag. "I haven't helped you with the dishes. Oh, dear, it *is* late. I'm sorry. Do you mind if I go?"

I hugged her and we held one another close, kissing each other on each cheek.

"No, no dear. I knew you had a date. Don't worry. When shall I see you? Tomorrow sometime?"

She thought for a minute. "Do you mind if we make it for dinner, not through the day? I want to finish something tomorrow, before we go away. Do you mind?"

"Of course not. Don't worry. I'm going to Belleville tomorrow and it takes all day. Come here when you can. I'll be here at dinnertime."

Again we embraced. She called to me before she got onto the elevator with her constant reminder, "Remember, don't sneak over to the Delaunay show without me," and the elevator door closed on her as I waved my hand in promise.

# 6

Tuesday was gray and the heat hung close to the ground. I could smell it as I came out of the building and walked the wide stairs to the cobbled pavement below. There was continuing construction going on around the large complex of which the apartments were only a part, and the broad walk leading to the street was a maze of tar vats and jackhammers and handcarts heavy to the brim with building materials. I walked around them, watching the slow-moving workmen in their blue shirts and black cotton pants. They looked like Turks or Algerians, and I kept bumping into them because they were moving in all the directions that seemed to be mine.

The smell of the tar in that heat and the heavy French cigarettes, the whiff of the morning's quick brandy and black coffee, the stench of the taxis and buses on the avenue itself, and somehow, everywhere, the impalpable odor that rose and mingled with it all, of the cheap scent of lavender, the subway scent of lavender, that particular Paris smell, made me burst out to myself: "I love Paris. For no reason, really, I just love it. The way Abby does."

A line out of an old movie popped into my head. Charles Boyer, Pepe le Moko, hiding out in the Casbah, touching the big blobby pearl earring on Hedy Lamarr's earlobe and saying in that tense, passionate Gallic accent of his, black eyes gleaming, his voice sick with longing for her and home: "All that *chichi*—and you remind me of the Métro."

Abby had again talked to me about my moving to Paris, when we were walking home from the market at Vanves on Saturday.

"What would I do here, darling?" was my answer. "If Daddy were still alive, maybe. But alone? I'd just be an aging lady alone in a big city." I paused, made melancholy by my own words. "No. It's too late."

"But I'm here," she said, squeezing my arm, which was interlocked with hers.

"I don't think it's right to choose a place just because your child is here."

"Why not? It's not wrong. It's neither right nor wrong. Honestly, Mother, you're so determined not to get into your children's way, that you don't see it clearly. It would be good to have you close. You have some friends here, and my friends love you."

"That's dear of you to say so, Abby. But what would I do?"

Do? Now as I savored the Paris smell, I thought if I had the money I wouldn't do anything. I'd buy a little apartment and come and stay in Paris for two or three months each year, close to Abby, enjoying her, having time enough, when the inevitable irritations arose between us, to work them out directly, not in retrospect or by letter. Then I'd go back to my house in Connecticut and work and enjoy that too, because I did. It was the place Charles and I had loved so together and it was filled with him, every corner. I sighed; it would be the best of both worlds if I could swing it.

But hell, I thought, plunging into the labyrinth of the Montparnasse-Bienvenue subway station, I haven't the money for both. And I haven't the time. I just have these infrequent visits, once or twice each year. Still, I thought, what an essential part of my life! The feel of Abby, the idea of Abby, three thousand miles away, was a dimension in my daily living that filled the empty crevices of the day and night with warmth.

I hopped onto the moving electric walk in the subway. It seemed to stretch through all of Paris underground, rolling interminably from one end of the station to the other. I clung to the right-hand rail. There was always an endless file of walkers who raced on the belt, impatient with the set speed. I just stood there, taking it at its own pace, reading the posters on the wall as we passed, poster after poster, all the same; the medium is the message, I thought, non-stop hammer blows, get it, get it.

"I have to live where I can make it on my own," I continued my conversation with myself as I moved ahead motionlessly, my camera bag at my feet. "Abby is with me every day, the sense of her is with me every day, my house at home is full of her, too, her paintings, all her crazy gifts to me through the years. I don't have to live in Paris to be near her," but suddenly my heart leaped as I thought of it. *No*, I put down the idea. "It's the same with Debby. There's no one more sustaining. And John, my funny, profound John. Would I live in Ottawa? Or L.A.? No. I know my place."

Debby had once argued with me my belief that parents should stay out of the way as long as possible as they grew older.

"That's nonsense, Mother." She had been forthright. "I don't agree with you at all. I certainly can see a time when you'll want to come live with me. In the same house, or in a place of your own nearby. It's only natural."

I'd never forgotten her words. Even in my stubborn independance, I had to admit they were comforting. I sighed as I jumped off the moving belt. An open life, the right to choose, options—these were the province of the young. They were unwanted riches for me.

At last I was on the train headed in the direction of Châtelet, another of those interminable stations, where I changed for the line headed for the Porte des Lilas. I underestimated where I wanted to get off and came onto the street at the Belleville station. I fiddled in my bag and brought out my camera, which I slung around my neck. The sultry gray mist still clung to the lower air, and the high reach of the Rue de Belleville rose before me like the crest of a punishing hill. I had forgotten how steep it was and that the stop on the subway that I should have taken was toward the top of the rise.

"Well," I thought, "I'm not going back down into the subway. I'll walk it."

I really dragged it, in a kind of dismay. Monique had been right. There was change everywhere. Big modern poured-concrete apartment complexes all along the left-hand side as I climbed. The right side of the street still had its little shops, the butcher, the baker, but all with the iron shutters down. August was taken seriously in this part of town; the traditional annual closing was a ritual.

I was extremely tired as I walked up and up. There wasn't a single photograph I wanted to take. My camera hung like a millstone. The shoulder bag weighed a ton. I felt sad and lonely, bereft. I didn't quite know why. This had been an expedition I had planned for a long time. Indeed, when the Paris apartment for the month had been offered me, I had written Abby enthusiastically, telling her there was a book I had in mind centered on Belleville; and I assured her that I wouldn't be in her way, there was no need to entertain me, I welcomed the chance to do my own leisurely research.

There was a café at the corner of the Avenue Bolivar and I sat outside at one of the little rattan tables that poked its way onto the sidewalk. It wasn't a terrace, just a few tables, and I sat waiting for the waiter, rather glad that he was slow in coming so I could just sit. Everything looked unfamiliar. I had remembered a rushing slum, vibrant with color and young people, clusters of old women with their loaded shopping bags gathering to talk, mostly in Yiddish during those years when I first came here—French Yiddish, Bronxian as the English Yiddish but somehow more amusing to my ear.

Now it was quiet. Was it a combination of August and Auschwitz? I wondered. The few young people who passed looked like young people everywhere—blue jeans, T-shirts, long hair, and boots. No, not everywhere, I smiled to myself. "Only in France, I thought, would there be high boots in the summer."

I went into the café finally and asked the young man at the counter for a large coffee-cream to take out to the table outside. The proprietor, obviously the father, saw me and exploded at his son for not having served me at the little table. If I would be good enough, he waved to me, to make

myself comfortable outside, of course his son would serve
me there immediately. I hadn't remembered such politesse
in the Belleville I knew. Well, why not? I went back outside,
which meant almost toward the curb of the cross streets
where the little outdoor tables were perched, and sat down
again.

"It will be good to be in the country after all," I thought.
"It's just as well we're leaving tomorrow." The city, from this
viewpoint, so unlike my memory of it, seemed bleak and
unrewarding. It had a nameless, faceless look. It didn't
check out.

After the large, good coffee and a cigarette, I gathered up
my gear and continued my climb. There were fewer new
buildings here than down below, but still the very air was
unfamiliar. More had changed than buildings.

At the Place Jourdain, with its trim and tidy church and
the patisserie shop on the corner, I recognized the Métro
stop I should have used. But even this very familiar corner
had an unfamiliar air. I crossed the square to look at the
cake shop and, wonder of wonders, it was open. I went in
and bought an apple tart to eat on the way. Such a neat, luxurious cake shop. As formal and well-displayed as any such
shop in any part of town. It had the smug air of a good
neighborhood cake shop in a good, solid neighborhood. Certainly not a cake shop for a slum or a poor quarter. Was this
only façade, I wondered. Or had the slum vanished with
the ghetto?

On a corner a bit farther up the hill, I saw the building
donated by the Rothschilds to help "the Hebrews find a better place for themselves in France." I read the inscription
carefully, the past sweeping through me like an arctic wind,
icy with foreboding. Farther ahead was the tenement I was

seeking, where my aunt and all my cousins had lived for so many years. I passed it by, not recognizing it, and was suddenly aware that I had gone too far.

I walked back. It was there. It looked the same but seemed smaller and cleaner. The courtyard had no clothes hanging across its cobbled stones, there were no noisy children, no old men with prayer shawls around them, not even any cats. The water faucet, which had once been the only running source for the whole house, looked rusted and unused.

I didn't recognize a single name on the wall bell board. No Polish endings. No Germanic twists. No shortened reminders of the Eastern steppes. I turned and walked down the hill to the subway and took the long ride back to the Montparnasse apartment and collapsed on the couch, crying frantically, foolishly, for no reason I could articulate, even in an inchoate way, to myself. I was just undone.

"Oh, Charles, darling. Charles. Charles. I miss you so." He would have understood my grief. I would not have had to explain to him about my Tante Molly and my cousin Annette and those missing names.

I fell asleep, and it was dark again when I awoke. Again I was frantic. Where were my glasses? What time was it? Where was Abby? When she arrived, at eight-thirty, I was so glad to see her, I held her close in the open doorway, blocking her entrance. Her arms came around me tightly.

"Don't worry, Mummy. Don't worry, Mummy. Everything will be all right." She didn't move me back into the room. She didn't ask any questions. She just held me and hugged me and repeated in that special, soft, love-choked voice she sometimes used with me, "Don't worry, Mummy, please don't worry. It's all right."

I washed my face and put on some fresh makeup while

she smoked and talked, calling to me from the living room while I repaired the damages of the day, in the bathroom.

"I had a tremendous day, Mummy. I really worked. There were some things I wanted to do with that new painting, even before I blocked in the background, and I did them. Then I did a black-and-white drawing of the heads again. I've been concerned about the shape of the large head in the middle. I think I have it right now. I'm glad."

I came out of the bathroom and looked at her, tucked in against the pillows of the couch, her blue legs bright beneath the skirt of the black dress. She shone. Her face was flushed, not in the angry, allergic way that happened when the blood ran up the wrong track, but illuminated. Her enormous eyes looked as blue-green as her stockings and the bright, wedged, matching shoes. "You look wonderful, darling. Hungry?"

"Famished. I haven't had a thing since breakfast—oh, maybe a tomato, but nothing else." She stretched comfortably. "I love to go out first thing in the morning to buy croissants and cigarettes, it wakes me up, but after I get started, I'd rather starve than leave."

"Let's go, then. I'm ready."

She unwound herself, stood up, and then, suddenly, caught me close. "I understand. I do. I know how you feel. But I warned you about Belleville. It's gone. It's another place."

I rested my head on her shoulder, consoled by her. "It isn't only that," I mumbled.

She kissed my forehead. "I know you miss Daddy." The tears started in my eyes again. "It isn't the same for me as for you, Mummy, I know that. Yours is a day-to-day sadness; you miss having him to talk to, every day, about everything. But don't we share something about him, Mummy, don't we? We always have."

We went hand in hand around the corner of the building and toward the lights of Montparnasse. The crowds were enormous, the traffic zooming in and out around the avenues that met at the corner of the boulevard and the Rue de Rennes. It was warm and gay and we decided to go again to Chez Rougeot, because it had been so good on Sunday. Crossing the street toward the restaurant took the fine art of dodging. Cars seemed to be coming at us from all directions. Abby pushed me back at one point, when I started weaving my way between cars.

"Don't do that, Mother; be careful. You have to watch it, go with the lights along the hammered line. All French drivers are idiots. You take your life in your hands."

She guided me across the broad passage and we laughed when we arrived at the other side, in front of the restaurant. "At last," she said, "arrived. Only New Yorkers jay-walk. Parisians know they haven't a chance."

"That's odd from you," I countered. "You used to drive me wild at the way you crossed the street, never looking."

"Well, that wasn't Paris. And I don't want you hurt." She held my arm close to her body. "Dear old Mummy."

The outside terrace of the restaurant was crowded. There would be no table for us, this night, on the street. Inside, some people were just leaving, getting up from a table at the front of the restaurant. It was not as much fun as the open café, nor as the gay old part in the rear, but we took possession of the table eagerly anyway.

"Lucky," Abby said. "This is just the time when the queue starts forming, wait and see. Better take what we can get now."

"It's not bad. And we can watch the crowd coming in. I love to watch."

We were tucked into the first table against the wall, separated from the door by an etched-glass partition. The old mirror on the opposite wall was mottled and the silvered back shone through. The reflections it caught were distorted and wavy, like reflections under water.

"This is good." I settled back comfortably. "I only had an apple tart and a coffee myself."

"Where?"

"I bought the tart in a pastry shop in front of the Jourdain Métro stop. I ate it on the street."

"On the street, hmm. There are lots of blacks and Arabs up there now, did you know? Not where you were. Towards the Rue Bisson. They say the blacks have a village system. The Senegalese on one side, the Nigerians on another. It's interesting but dangerous. I wouldn't go alone if I were you, eating an apple tart on the street."

"Abby!" I protested, amused at her instructing me.

"I know Paris better than you do."

I reached over and caught her hand. "I'm not going back. It's all in my mind. The part I care about. Let's order," I closed the discussion.

We went through the menu. "Let's eat a lot," I said. "We don't know what we'll find on the trip."

"Are you mad? Burgundy! It's famous for food. And Claude has given us a special list of places." She beamed. "Won't it be fun? The country. Green. Let's plan to drive above Dijon, too. There's nothing much there, nothing for touring, but just some wonderful, wide-open farms, some old towns, just lovely expanses of green and gold."

"That sounds good. Are there places to stay?"

Abby shrugged. "Who knows? We'll take our chances. But it will be worth it. It's so beautiful there. I've thought about going back for a long time."

"We might go to Beaune, for old time's sake. You've never seen the Hospice."

"Okay. Lovely. Beaune? Daddy loved it there, didn't he?"

"He loved sampling the wine there," I said, and we both smiled. "He did, really. We took the car for a trip down the Côte d'Or and stopped at every vineyard for a taste. When we got back to Beaune that night, he was loaded. The Hôtel de la Poste wasn't as smart then as it is now, and when we stayed there, it was quite cozy. That night, Daddy insisted on dinner in the dining room, and the waiter knew enough to tuck us into a corner. He ordered *coq au vin* in Chambertin wine and then more wine in those big balloon glasses they used to use, maybe they still do—anyway, he was drunk as a monkey by the time we crawled upstairs." I stopped, then added, "But he wasn't bad."

"Did he bellow 'Roll Over, Mabel'?" she asked.

"No. I don't remember. I think he went quietly."

We both smiled at Charles's old R.A.F. song, rollicking and obscene and somehow extremely personal to him. We were silent as we remembered it, looking at the menu while the waiter stood, pencil in hand, unhurried although a longish line had already formed in front of the door. Abby again did the ordering. Her usual herring in cream, roast lamb, white beans, salad. I, the roast chicken with watercress, not too heavy, mindful of the Burgundian food to come.

Abby lit a cigarette. "I do wish that John and Patti had been able to be with us that day, singing 'Mabel.' I thought about it later. I really wished it."

Again we were quiet. "It's rather sad, isn't it," she said, "that only tragedy brings people back together again. How many years since I'd seen John? Years and years. And we were so close growing up."

"I know. So close, like twins almost, twin monkeys."

"It's not only our closeness in age, I remember. We were close-close, Mummy. We were one another." Her eyes flooded with tears. "I've often wondered what happened. How we became separated."

"Time. Space. This hateful mobile society." I tried to be comforting.

"No. It was more than that." Again silence. "Philippe was lousy to John. I couldn't help it."

"Forget it," I said. "It's in the past."

She had a habit of dragging deeply on her cigarette when she was perturbed or nervous. She had a number of mannerisms with cigarettes—flirtatious, intense, childlike, sophisticated—and this particular, agitated, deep pull, as if dragging in strength.

"It was very special for me to see him again. He's like Daddy, you know."

"In a way," I agreed, "but not really."

"Yes, he is. I listened to him and watched him, with all those people coming and going, relatives, strangers. John was marvelous, so urbane, able to talk to everyone. And so damn clever, his jokes like Daddy's, so you could understand them or not, there were plays on words, on ideas, and if you got them, great—if not, no harm, you never knew the difference."

"He's very witty, sharp-minded, acute," I agreed. "And he's a serious man, too, you know. He's had a lot of problems. I wish Daddy had known, before he died, how John

was meeting them." I was quiet now too, then went on.
"One thing John said to me I shall never forget: We were
alone, private for a moment in Daddy's room, hiding from
all the rush around us. I told him how sorry I was that he
hadn't gotten into medical school. He put his arm around
me and said, 'It's okay. It was an idea, a possibility. But I've
learned one thing, it's how to deal with failure.'"

"Dear John." Again Abby's eyes flooded with tears. "He
would have made a good doctor, but I'm glad that's over. I
hate doctors." With good reason, I thought. Then she burst
into laughter, loud enough to make people at the next table
look up. She clapped her hand over her mouth like a little
girl. "I laugh too loud," she confessed, peering through her
lashes around the restaurant, "but I just remembered a joke
Daddy told me when I visited him in the hospital one time.
About the man in the white coat pushing his way through
the queue trying to get into Heaven. St. Peter lets him in
and everyone in line complains. 'Who the hell does he think
he is?' says someone. 'Sh-sh,' says another, 'don't you know?
That's God playing doctor.'"

"That's a Daddy joke," I laughed. "Poor guy. He had his
share."

"Did he want John to be a doctor?" she asked.

I shrugged. "I don't know. I don't know if I did either. It
seemed a long way from Berkeley and Chaucer and poetry
readings at the local saloon, which John had started with.
But, you know, Daddy was acutely aware of the loneliness
and uncertainty of being a writer. 'Sal métier,' he would say,
quoting Flaubert. Perhaps he felt that there would be secu-
rity for John if he were a doctor—a doctor like William
Carlos Williams, he used to say, combining the best of
both." I hesitated, thinking about it. "But it was John's own

idea, not any one else's. All we wanted is that he be able to do what he himself wanted."

We were almost finished with our dinner. We noticed, in the line waiting for tables, a girl wearing a skirt made of an old Spanish shawl, with all the fringe hanging tattered and torn. Another girl was wearing an old pink georgette chemise, completely naked beneath it.

"We used to call that a shimmy," I said.

"I thought that was a dance."

"It was American for *chemise,* I guess." My eyes were glued to the beautiful body clearly visible in every detail beneath the pink mist. "Maybe that's fashionable in New York now too, but I wouldn't know. I never go where you would see it, where the young gather."

"Young or old, here in Paris it's a matter of taste, not age."

I nodded in agreement. "Shall we have dessert?" I asked her.

"Yes, oh, yes, I was starved. I'm just beginning to feel right." We were looking at the dessert menu when I asked, almost involuntarily, "How was your evening last night? I hope you weren't too late getting back to your place."

Her face reddened and seemed suddenly stern. Damn it, I thought. I wish I didn't persist in this loaded question. She clung to her menu tightly. I felt her anger; but when she answered, she was quite controlled.

"It was fine. Jean was worried. His mother is ill. He left early."

"Oh, I'm sorry," I said, trying to fill the gap between us that my question had caused.

After the waiter took our dessert order, she decided to go on with it. "I spoke to Jean about meeting you while you're here this time. We agreed. When you and I come back from Burgundy, perhaps we'll have dinner, the three of us."

"I'm glad," I said. "It would really make things more natural."

She bristled. "I don't know what you mean by natural, Mother. But we've agreed."

I said nothing more. It was she who added, "I hope it goes all right. I don't want any dissension. Debby and Jean were a disaster when they met."

I was edgy. "That's not so, Abby. Why do you say so?"

"Well, it is so. You know it. Didn't she tell you?"

"She didn't say much," I hedged. Debby had said that Jean was thorny, possessive. I didn't intend to repeat it.

"Well, what did she say?" When Abby was aroused to questioning, she hammered away at it. "Did she like him? What did she say?"

"Let me think. She said one thing." I tried for the easiest truth. "She said he was very good-looking."

Abby pounded the table in disgust. "What a thing to say! What's that to say about anybody? Who cares about that?"

"But, Abby, she was only describing him," I protested. But how plain was Jean's importance to her! How passionately she wanted him loved and protected and admired! How defensive she was! I remembered something else Debby had said. I repeated it now. "Debby said that you were both almost like brother and sister, so protective of one another. She said you told her that he was your best friend."

She was close to tears. She shook her head sadly. "I don't know why I'm always so tense about this, Mother. I really don't. Jean is close to my heart, he is my flesh and blood. But he is difficult, he does have moods, he's so often in despair. I'm torn between wanting to shield him and then feeling I'm not going to let it get me down."

"But, Abby, my darling," I said. "What is so unusual about that? Just think. It's not an emotional climate either of us are unfamiliar with."

She nodded at me, suddenly quieted. "You mean you and Daddy, don't you? I know that."

She grabbed my hand and held it.

"It would have been easier," I said, trying to make it lighthearted, "if he had been an insurance agent. But he wasn't." I fiddled with my cup of coffee, drank it down. "You learn these things. I cannot believe my luck in having had your father for almost forty years. When I think of it, Abby, in spite of everything, I am the most fortunate of women to have had him—warts and all." I laughed. "Of course, there were a million times I didn't think so—" and she laughed with me.

We walked back to the apartment house, threading our way through the crowds on all the sidewalks leading home. When we came to the staircase leading up to the building's ramp, we embraced, kissing both cheeks. "I'll pick up the car by nine-thirty. I'll be at your place about twenty after ten. Let's get a good start."

"Why don't I come here?" she offered. "It might be easier that way. Then you won't have to come through the traffic."

"No." I waved her offer aside. "It will be easier for you. And then we can get right on the Périphérique at the Porte d'Orléans and be on our way."

"Yes, it does make sense," she agreed and gave me another hug. "Bravo! We're off to the country."

"Be ready," I warned, "there's no place to park on your street."

"I'll be ready."

"Ha ha."

"I will. You'll see." And I lost sight of her as I mounted the stairs set into the wall blocking the view as she ran down the avenue to the subway.

# 7

---

"Of course the car is ready," said the young man at the Europecar office when I showed up the next morning. But he fussed and fussed with the forms; did I want insurance? total or not total? credit card? driver's license? Then I asked him whether Route National Five was in good condition. How did he know? He had only questions. No answers.

Finally the young man was finished with the forms, left his desk to go to the back of the garage and drove the little car forward. I got in. He snapped directions at me. Here the windshield wipers, that button for the lights, turn this around in that direction and you had high, this direction, low, the horn here. The instructions were concluded bambam and he was gone with a *"Bon voyage."* It flashed through my mind, as it always did when I went through this process on a rented car, that there was absolutely no check on one's ability to drive this particular vehicle. I pushed the clutch in clumsily, tried to find my way into first gear, finally did with a bit of lurching, and was out of the garage, wondering where second gear was, and decided to stay in it, if I ever found it, through the crowded streets. By the time I hit the Avenue du Maine, my ancient memories of the stick shift returned and I was able to make my way, bumping along.

It was twenty minutes past ten when I drove into Abby's street and honked beneath her window. She opened the shutters and looked down impatiently. I couldn't see whether she was dressed or not, but I caught the flash of bright clean blue.

"You're early, Mother," she called down irritably. "You said ten-thirty. I'm just not ready."

I was irritated in my own turn but kept it in check. I didn't want to get started in the wrong mood. I pulled the car to the curb, illegally, and decided to wait without reproach. She was downstairs in about five minutes, her face worried.

"I'm all ready, Mother, but I'm trying to defrost the refrigerator. Why don't you come up? I hate to keep you waiting."

She, too, was eager to start off cheerfully. Keeping me waiting was a mother-daughter rite between us, but this time she wanted all to go smoothly.

"Don't worry," I told her cheerfully. "Take your time. I'm very illegal here. I'll just sit until you're ready."

"Okay, Mummy." She leaned in and gave me one of her suckling kisses on the cheek. "I'll bring down what I have in the fridge. We can eat on the way."

"Why defrost the fridge at all?" I called to her as she headed toward her entrance hall.

"Ten days of electricity," she called back. "Are you kidding?"

So she was looking forward to a ten-day holiday. I was pleased, happy, and then furious, because it was twenty minutes before she was down again. I controlled my anger. That was Abby. Careless of time, unaware of its passage; whatever had delayed her now? But here she was, a small bag in one hand, a basket in another, and when we opened the trunk to put in her things, she chided me, as she always did, at the amount of luggage that was there. We tucked in her little bag with mine. Then she held up a couple of worn-looking tomatoes, a peach, and a small blob of cheese out of her basket.

"Couldn't let this go to waste. We'll lunch on the way."

"Or throw them out," I joked as I snapped the luggage compartment closed.

She stood at the side of the car before she got in. "You haven't said anything about the way I look." She twirled around.

"You didn't give me a chance, with those tomatoes and the peach."

She pirouetted around on the curb. "This is one of the things I bought with my Christmas money. See?" It was the pretty blue cotton shift I had seen in her closet, and she was wearing it over a dazzling white shirt. She held out her sleeve. "See the white, see it?" She was like a child in her eagerness. I touched the white collar above the blue shift, ran my finger along the exquisite, hand-drawn fagoting.

"It's beautiful," I said. "I love it."

"You don't recognize it? It's the nightshirt you bought me at the place in Les Halles. Remember? You insisted." She was triumphant.

I remembered. I had loved the drawn work and urged the old lawn nightshirt on her. It was during one of our days wandering around the remnants of Les Halles, after the market had fled to Rungis but before all the ironwork sheds had been torn down. It had been a ravishing day together. I remembered it very well. I touched the white collar again. "It's enchanting. And so span clean."

"It washes like a handkerchief. Don't you love it with this blue?"

I nodded.

"I've been saving it to wear today. I knew you'd love it." Then she chided me. "Why didn't you say right away that you loved it? I bet you never noticed it."

She got into the car and I started the motor. I couldn't say to her that I didn't mention the blue and white because I was aware of how worn and tired Abby looked this morning. The rouge stood out plainly on her white cheeks. Her eyes were paler blue than usual, troubled by the sunlight. I thought, being with me every single day must be tiring—not tiresome, but tiring. She had always guarded her privacy, her aloneness. I wanted to reach out and touch her. Instead I started the car.

"I had to turn off the gas on the shower, too," she said as we rocked into the street off the curb. She waved to Madame Goby, the concierge, who called, *"Bon voyage,"* to us. She called, *"Bon jour,"* to another neighbor as we passed. "I'm sorry I kept you waiting. But I didn't want the gas on and I checked the valves on the stove. Then I wanted to stack one of my pictures behind the drawing board—"

I stopped her. I was no longer irritated. What difference did it make? "We're off on a holiday, love, what does it matter if we leave ten minutes late?"

She settled back contentedly.

"Do you mind if we go to the post office?" I said. I had written some letters the night before and I wanted to mail them.

"No. I need cigarettes, too."

We turned into the Rue d'Alésia, toward the post office. She dashed out of the car to the P.T.T., her blue dress flying. I noticed that the white nightshirt hung below the dress.

"It would look better not showing," I thought. "Maybe I'll tell her later on." Then I caught myself. Abby had her own ideas about dress. The white showed beneath the blue hemline because she wanted it to. And I warned myself, "For heaven's sake, don't tell her she looks pale and tired. If she doesn't feel well, it will only make her feel worse."

On the corner, a few doors from the post office, was a to-bacco shop. I inched the car toward the corner and watched her cross the street. "She's so sad-looking." I felt the spasm of concern that always shook me with her. "So beautiful and sad."

But when she got into the car, her smile was wide and in-fectious. "That old man in the *tabac*," she laughed. "He chided me for the three packs. 'You're too young to smoke so much,' he said, 'even if I shouldn't say it. It's my profit.'" She shook her head happily. "Everyone around this area is so concerned. They recognize you. They know you're a per-son. Even if it is their profit, you're a person."

I made the right turn down into the avenue toward the Porte d'Orléans, sputtering and stalling. "I'm sorry. I'm not great on the shift thing. I'll get it soon."

She looked down at the seat on her left. "Isn't the brake on?"

I felt for it. It was. "What a fool!" I exclaimed as we now forged smoothly ahead. "Thank you, Abby. What a fool!"

She was terribly pleased, obviously pleased, that she had been helpful. She had gotten a driver's license in Massachusetts but had been so dreadful at it that she and we were relieved that never again, now that she had her "certificate," as she called it, would she drive. Consequently, she was usually illiterate about the habits and manners of the road and cars.

"We could have huffed and puffed all the way if you hadn't caught that. I'm used to the brake in another place. Thank you."

"Jean's brakes are in the same place. That's how I noticed it." She sat back, pleased with herself. Anything that proved her not totally inefficient in the mechanics of life pleased her. She lit a cigarette and closed her eyes.

"Tired?" I asked, glancing over at her.

She shook her head. "No. Not exactly." She was silent, watching me as we maneuvered the curves around toward the left and onto the speedway circling the city. She looked exhausted.

"I found an English copy of Mailer's book on Marilyn Monroe at the apartment. I read *at* it last night," I said, simply to make conversation. "I was surprised to see it there."

"Why surprised?" she asked. "Did you like it?"

"I simply couldn't understand why he would bother to write it. She was a nothing dame."

"You're quite wrong, Mother." Abby's voice was positive and sure, her fatigue dropping away from her in the spirit of an argument. "She wasn't a nothing dame. She was a terrible, self-centered, fragile egocentric, but the book's about Mailer, not about her, and it's about America, too. Anything he writes about is about America, and even when it's bad, it's vital and important."

I hadn't intended a discussion on Mailer as we wove our way through traffic. "I just wondered why the book was of interest to the French at all." One never knew, I thought, when a serious note with Abby would be struck. "We have to watch for the exit to National Five," I changed the subject. "Here's Claude's paper"; I fumbled for it beside me. "And here's the map." I thrust them both on her lap. "Help me watch."

She looked at the paper with the directions on it and folded it beneath her hands. She spoke slowly, still trying to explain why she had kept me waiting back at her apartment and her own sense of fatigue, which she knew I had noticed.

"The clinic is closed in August," she reminded me. "Madame goes away. I try to do my exercises at home. It isn't the same thing."

Her back, her pain—they burned through my consciousness. I wanted to reach over to her. She was so gay or sad or serious, or so childlike or so grave most of the time, that even I, so alert, so guilty, so worried about her scoliosis over so many years, sometimes forgot the pain. I did reach over to her now and touched her hand. "Perhaps we walked too much last night?"

Again she looked sad. "Who knows? I never know. It's just worse some nights than others." She dragged tensely at her cigarette. "It will be okay. I smoked last night. That helped."

Involuntarily I wondered if that was why she looked so drawn and her eyes a blue washed paler than usual? I felt uneasy. Of what? About what? Of her way of dealing with pain? What did I know about it? "It's too bad the clinic closes for such a long time." I spoke critically.

"Not so." She was immediately protective; the clinic was her sanctuary; she drove back any criticism. "They need a holiday. Everyone does. It can't be helped."

The traffic hemmed in and around us, some cars whizzing by, sampling each lane, in and out.

"I'll be glad to get off this insane road soon. Watch for the turning."

We saw it at the Porte de Pantin and swung off the speedway. It was suddenly familiar, not much changed for better or worse. The outskirts of Paris, dreary, provincial, three stories high, red brick and cement blocks. I noticed a subway stop. I hadn't realized the Métro went out so far.

"It must be cheaper to live out here. And easy enough to get into town."

She shuddered. "I'd rather live in the worst hole, the worst slum in Paris, than out here. Imagine it. It isn't even stony-faced Balzac country, with all kinds of concealed vileness behind the shutters."

"How do you know?" I laughed. "There's no telling."

"I know." She spoke decisively. "The vileness here would just be X-rated blue stuff. Nothing devious and monstrous and hidden, behind a decorous façade."

We left the suburbs and followed Five out into the country. The road was ugly and littered with billboards.

"I remember when this highway was bordered with trees," I told her. "Giant plane trees on each side. So beautiful."

"Why did they cut them down?"

"Road safety, they claimed. But I wonder if it wasn't the same reckless plunder of the landscape and the cities that

happened everywhere after the war. For no reason. Roch-
ester, New York, inner loops and outer loops. Urban re-
newal, auto safety, devastation."

We reached Fontainebleau and swung through the town,
intending to find a place to pick up some food for lunch.
Our plan was to eat picnic lunches at noon and save the big
splurge for the evening meal. But every curb in Fontainebleau was crowded, especially around the food stores,
and there was no place to park. We passed a likely-looking
*charcuterie*, and Abby suggested she run in while I double-
parked but I said no when I saw the line in front of the
store. "Let's not bother; we'll find something ahead."

There was nothing ahead, and soon we were on the open
road again. At a little village, which was only two long rows
of desultory buildings on each side of the highway, we spotted a bakeshop. By this time I was starved. I pulled up on
the curb while Abby went inside. Immediately, I was surrounded by a town outburst that I couldn't quite understand. A woman in her doorway across the road shook her
fist at me in anger.

"What the hell?" I thought. "What am I doing to her?"

Then some men poured out of the tavern beside the bakeshop and started yelling at me too. I hadn't the faintest idea
what my infraction was.

Abby heard the noise inside the store and came out with a
small package in white paper. "Let's go," she said.

"What are we doing wrong?" I asked, bewildered.

"We're on their fucking curb, I guess. Who knows?
Maybe it's holy ground."

I swung off and into the highway while Abby cheerfully
pointed two fingers upward at them in an obscene salute.

She unwrapped the white paper. "It was a lousy bakeshop

anyway. I didn't want to stop to look beyond the case. Here's what they had on the counter."

I reached over for a thick, doughy apple tart. "Ugh. Let's break our rule. It's our first day on holiday. Let's stop at Sens and lunch there."

She nodded. "I think we'd better or we'll have to do without. It's almost closing time for the stores."

The road became more rural. There were stretches of trees lining each side now. Not the great trees of the past, but as if, in protest, each individual farmer had staked trees along his side of the road to remind drivers of bygone felicity.

Abby sat back and sighed blissfully, drinking in the air. "I love these little hills. What simple curves they make over the land. They don't bump up. Just a gentle rise here and there. See."

"Beautiful country. We should see the Yonne soon."

"I like the way it feels to my eye," she murmured. "Do you know what I mean? It feels good to look at."

I nodded. This countryside was green and live yellow. Not parched, but juicy and fertile. We saw the white Charolais cattle grazing beside watered patches. "They couldn't have been much hit by the drought."

"According to *Le Monde,* everything was hit by the drought. The worst in a hundred years. But you can't see it here, I agree. I don't know why."

We saw the rise of Sens at the crest of the hill. "Good," I said. "Lunch. And Abby, I warn you. This place is famous. We must take some time to see the cathedral."

She snorted. She hated sight-seeing. "Must we? What's so famous about it?"

"I don't quite remember, you heel. It was the bishop's see

when Paris was a mudhole. We can look it up in the *Guide*.
But I remember it as famous."

"That means it will be full of tourists, Mother. But," she
added begrudgingly, "we can see."

I pulled up in the square in front of the cathedral and we
headed for one of the cafés alongside. It was past noon, but
the square was quite deserted. We had no difficulty finding
a table on the terrace in front of the café we chose. A waitress came out immediately and suggested sandwiches of the
house *paté*. We both agreed and ordered two large coffees
with milk.

The toilet was up two steep, dark flights of stairs, and we
took turns going there. When we were both finally settled at
the table, the food arrived, each sandwich a whole loaf of
fresh bread, a *baguette* slashed in half and loaded with *paté*.

"I'm hungry," I said, looking at the enormous length of
bread. "But I'll never manage this."

"But it's good," she said, plunging in eagerly. "It's a real
country *paté*."

Some young Japanese were sitting on the terrace next to
us, poring over their guidebooks and signaling to one another the items of interest in the book.

"They're like German tourists," Abby mumbled through
her mouthful. "Just ask them. They'll tell you what's
significant about the cathedral. How tall the columns. And
why they taper."

I pinched her beneath the table. "You may be a lousy
tourist, but some people are different."

"I know," she conceded. "You're like that, Mummy." She
smiled affectionately. "Every little fact has a meaning."

"Debby is like that too," I said defensively.

She snorted wickedly. "Oh, no she's not, Mummy. We

have a plan, Debby and I. When we're older, we plan to
travel everywhere around the world and not look at anything at all. We just intend to walk quietly on side streets
and say hello to people. We don't want to hurry or go into a
single museum or even get up early in the morning to get
started. We're not going to *go*. We're going to *be*. That's
how Debby and I plan to travel."

"You two are a pain," I said jokingly. "Places of interest
interest me. Anyway, Christopher and I love to sight-see, so
we'll dodder along without you."

Abby laughed loudly this time. "I know. Debby told me
how you and Chris, your Pevsners in hand, kept comparing
notes all along the road to Bath. See—" she waved her hand
around the square airily. "Look. I'm sitting here and I love
it. Why should I go into that dreary-looking cathedral? I
know it's there. I can see it from here."

"How do you know?" I protested. "You loved Chartres."

"Yes. But Chartres is different. Chartres is—Chartres." She
paused in thought, suddenly deep within herself. She spoke
reflectively, weighing each word as if it were forbidden.
"That late afternoon, that dusky afternoon we were together
at Chartres, I shall never forget it." She sat rigidly upright
as she spoke. I felt her gravity charge through me. "Chartres
is the living God. There is a spirit there. I felt it. I knew it.
I'll never forget it. That fantastic rise above you, that upward reach. And the color, it was on fire, those windows lit
by the setting sun. I felt a leap. A leap of belief. I don't
know. A sense of presence beyond myself, where we were,
who we were." She shook her head to silence herself. It was
difficult to speak of faith, as if it were taboo.

I remembered, as she spoke, that two years earlier, she
had asked for a good copy of the King James Bible.

"I'll find one," I promised, and did, sending it off to her without questioning why. There was indeed no need to question why. It was just a book to have around, to read aloud, to roll on the tongue. All that sonorous, portentous poetry, familiar and everyday, yet magnificent.

"It should be in everyone's library, like the dictionary," I told Abby. But I caught a feeling then—and now again—of I didn't know what. That perhaps there was more than the literary in Abby's mind.

Out on the terrace, at the table in front of us, was a woman, well dressed in the way that Frenchwomen of a certain age and class always dress when they leave the house: a fine silk scarf knotted at the throat in the loose yet controlled way no one else ever manages, a tailored dark blue skirt, white blouse, beautifully polished leather shoes. She was with a child, a little girl, her grandchild perhaps, who kept leaning down beside her chair to poke her fingers into a basket on the ground next to her. She kept looking up at us as she poked and giggled.

Suddenly, in the midst of her memories of Chartres, Abby clutched my arm in delight. "Mummy, look. Look at that marvelous pussycat there."

The child eyed Abby with a wide smile, as if they had discerned one another.

Abby spoke to her in French. "That marvelous kitty-cat. Let me see it."

She left the table and knelt next to the child, and both of them poked their fingers in the basket, lifted the lid to miaow and singsong at the big, gray, shapely head that cocked its way up. The two of them, the child and Abby, babbled together in a private joy, and the waitress, who came out to watch, smiled with pleasure. When Abby rose to return to the table, she was pink with happiness.

"Did you see that cat's face, Mummy, did you see it? What an enormous head! Egyptian. Magnificent." She pushed the rest of her sandwich away from her and sighed voluptuously. "Oh, what a beautiful sight!"

While we were drinking the last of our coffee, I noticed a half-timbered house on the other side of the square, at the farthest corner. There was a dull-looking clothing store at street level, but above it was some timbering on the stone that looked medieval.

"Look at that," I pointed it out. "I wonder if it's truly old or fake."

Abby lifted her brows in a kind of bored irritation, rolling her eyes upward. "What difference does it make?" I could almost hear her say. "Here's the greatest cat in the world and she's concerned with a half-timbered house."

"Okay, Abby, so you're not interested," I said, with my own flash of annoyance, "but no need to make that face."

She was immediately penitent, eager to share my curiosity. "I don't know if it's old, Mother. It's probably real."

I turned to the waitress and asked if the corner building was fourteenth or fifteenth century. "Oh, old," she said. "Older than that."

"It's old indeed," suddenly the man at the table toward our right joined in the conversation. He spoke in English, haltingly. "You're American, aren't you?" he asked me. I nodded. "My wife speaks excellent English. She's upstairs now, but she would like to talk to you. She'll be right down. The building there is old, but there are others in the town, older still and very interesting. My wife will tell you about them."

"Oh, Mummy," breathed Abby, her face clouding. I pushed her, beneath the table.

"How good of you!" I said. "But we're just going."

"Please." He reached his hand out in air as if to hold us back. "My wife would love to speak English with you. She doesn't get much chance."

There was no stopping this without being rude. I again nudged Abby, under the table. "It might all be worth a few minutes' time," I whispered.

She shook her head at me balefully. But it was too late. Here was the wife. Her husband rose and brought her to us and we were pinned down. She was very beautiful in a solemn sort of way, perfect makeup, elegantly coifed, her hair a black, shining cap cut in the newest, oval fashion. Her costume of blue jeans and matching jacket was enormously smart. She was carrying one of the current brand-name bags, initials splashed all over the denim. She had the air of a somewhat mature, properly brought-up university student, good family, serious. I could feel Abby cringe at the total perfection. I was a bit uneasy too, eager now to be off and on our way but with no technique for evasion.

"Perhaps I can help you," she said. "Let me tell you about the cathedral. You have been in it, no?"

"No, not yet," I said.

"It is built like the cathedral at Canterbury. I'm sure you will notice this at once." I could feel Abby's fingernails up and down my thigh. "And Thomas à Becket—there is a memorial to him there. As for half-timbered houses, this one on the corner is not important at all. It is not good. If you walk down that street directly in front, perhaps a quarter of a mile you'll find a superb example."

She looked at Abby and repeated some of this in French.

Abby grinned slyly. "Oh, I understand English. Perfectly," she said. "I speak it too."

"Oh, you do? Yes. You speak English very well. Where did you learn?"

Abby smiled again, mischievously. "From my mother, here."

"Your mother." The young woman looked surprised. "But I thought you were French." She seemed confused. Abby was pleased, as it always pleased her to be taken for French; and pleased now to be making a dent in the young woman's pomposity.

"It surprises everyone to find she's my daughter," I said. The young woman really did look put out, and she had been trying to be nice and friendly. There was no sense being mean about it. "Where did you learn your English?" I asked her. "You speak extraordinarily well."

"At the Sorbonne," she said, "and at the *lycée* before that, of course."

"Of course."

She was warming to her task. She sat down in her chair at the next table and pulled it forward to join ours. Her husband interrupted her about an errand and took off. He was obviously delighted at this opportunity for her to speak to us and practice her English. He looked proprietary, as if he had arranged it all. She waved good-by to him cheerily. I was one with Abby now in hoping it would be a brief encounter.

"We're from Perpignan," she said. "We're making a little tour of France in this Morvan region. It's so historic."

I nodded. The blue of Abby's eyes watered over. She looked tired again, not eager to join in. She always seemed to fade in the hot air of this kind of talk.

"Perpignan is historic too," I said, "and I love the town near it—Céret, I think it is—where Maillot came from." I felt that I was helping extend this cultural chitchat. I wished I knew how to cut it short. It would irk Abby; her face showed it.

"This cathedral"—the young woman waved her hand toward the huge bulk of the twelfth-century St.-Étienne—"is not so beautiful as Chartres. And it is now being renovated, so you can't go in the front doors, but they're very fine, those doors. You will see."

She couldn't be stopped. "You have a very good writer," she continued, indicating by her tone a current best seller, "I mean an American. He has written very well on the French cathedrals, especially on Chartres."

I thought and thought. Whom could she mean? "Henry Adams?" I asked, somehow his name popping into my head. *"Mont-Saint-Michel and Chartres?"*

"Exactly," she said, pleased to have hit the nail squarely. "It is he. Exactly. I read him with joy."

Well, that was quite a current best seller for a casual café exchange. "We were just talking about Chartres, my daughter and I." I was by now embarrassed and bored.

The young woman turned to Abby as if to include her, but Abby's face turned scarlet. Our conversation about Chartres had been private. I could feel her stiffen. We had been talking about quite a different Chartres, about something else altogether, about a personal and singular response. Abby wanted no parallels with the responses of others, certainly not with the known and literary ones. The feelings she had shared with me were not to be shown off.

Abby was always sensitive to having her words repeated, to being quoted. "If I want to say things again, Mummy, I'll say them," she had once chided me. "Don't quote me in front of me as if I were unable to speak for myself, like an inarticulate child. Maybe I don't want to say the same thing to one person that I do to another."

I remember I had then apologized to her and offered as explanation the fact that she sometimes became so silent, clamming up tightly, that perhaps I tried to speak for her.

"Well, don't," had been her rejoinder. "I can manage on my own to say my say, when I want to say it."

And I remembered that she followed up her snappish response with a burst of laughter. "You're afraid people will think I'm an idiot, ha ha," and made her crazy idiot's face at me, pulling her lips down with one hand, lifting her eyes until only the whites showed and waggling out her tongue as she made her idiot noises.

"Marcel Marceau." I made her stop. "Your face will freeze that way and you'll be sorry."

The man from Perpignan returned and we were at last able to shake hands all around, express our delight in having encountered one another, and leave the café.

I whispered to Abby, "We'll have to go down the street to see that half-timbered house or her feelings will be hurt."

"You get yourself into these situations too easily, Ma," she said, tucking her arm into mine, "but why not? Let's go. It's not far."

So we walked arm in arm down the little street, which was also National Five, until we found the historic building. It was a square house with a colonnaded porch and the half-timber had been elaborated with some sculptured gargoyles at one side and the other. There were shops below and a plaque on the second story with the building's history.

"So okay, we've seen it," said Abby flatly. "Very interesting." She steered me back across the street. "Honestly, Mother, you and your social niceties; it's a bore. Now let's go see that Canterbury church or you'll never forgive me, and then let's be on our way if we want to get beyond Avallon while it's still light."

We made our way back up the street, looking at the shop windows filled with the same old things as the Rue d'Alésia, and then we were at the cathedral. It was chilly inside, forbidding, and in about one minute Abby said, "Come on. Let's go. It's better to read about than to see."

"Canterbury?" she asked as we found our way through the entry.

"Who knows? I've never been."

Her laughter rang through the doors as we found ourselves in the sunshine again. "You fraud." She clutched me with delight. "You nodded when our Perpignan lady made that architectural point."

"Only to show I was listening." I laughed too. "I was trying to be agreeable."

"That's what I mean."

We found our way to the parked car. "I hope she's not looking to see how long our little tour took."

Abby peeked slyly around the square. "No sign. Relax."

As she settled into the front seat of the Simca and I plunged and lurched forward, going from first to second and then onto the highway, Abby said, "She was a handsome woman, wasn't she?"

I nodded agreement.

"Imagine her luck finding an American tourist who knew the current American writer she was talking about." She paused. "Henry Adams. Sometimes I wish I knew more."

"You know a lot, Abby."

"I know some things. But I wish I knew more about ordinary things, like Henry Adams, for example."

"He really isn't that ordinary."

She was very grave. She didn't want to be put off by my assurances. "That woman, that kind of person leans on what they know. I sometimes wish I had more to lean on."

I turned my head to catch a glimpse of her face. It looked set, and I sensed a hungry sadness in her. Dear Abby, I thought, hungry always and yet, more than anyone else I knew, able to devour and savor and articulate in words, in touch, in work, her whole world around her. When she first tasted halvah, she called it cement candy. The time she wriggled under the coffee table in the living room and found it was painted blue underneath, she said, "I want to live in that blue." The light of the avenue around her old apartment had poured over her like honey. She breathed in the cold air and it crushed her bones. She breathed the warm air and it smelt like pain.

She turned to me now and her smile was radiant again. "I just wish I knew more because I wish I knew more—more and more and more. Not out of envy for anyone. Sometimes I think Debby is so brilliant, it dazzles me. But my life is my life and it's just the way I want it."

We were in deep country and it was beautiful. There was a road sign to the right marked VÉZELAY, 11 KM. "Abby, look. Vézelay. Shall we detour?"

"No. Let's keep going. It's almost five o'clock and you know we don't have a reservation."

"I guess you're right. But we'll come back. Maybe tomorrow. Don't you love Vézelay?"

"I do. It's not some cold cathedral. You can feel the whole

thing in your bones when you're there. We can come back tomorrow. Start our own Children's Crusade."

The sign for Avallon loomed ahead. "I'll be glad to be set for the evening. I think I'll nap before dinner. Oh, God, suppose there's no place."

"Don't let's worry. Claude was positive they would be able to find room at his inn. It's not exactly the Riviera."

We drove slowly through the town of Avallon. "There's a famous restaurant here," I told her. "Very expensive. We'll have to come back to look. Maybe we'll splurge."

"I love good places," she said. "Jean does too. Good food places. I can't stand them if they're just chic."

There was a big birthday cake in the window of a shop on the corner as we stopped to make a turn.

"That reminds me," Abby said. "How was Grandma's birthday party? Did you suffer too much?"

I told her as we spun down the highway, recounting the details, and we were laughing as I embroidered on them, pressed by her questions and her own observations, caustic and merry at the same time.

"We were all there, seventeen or eighteen at dinner. Aunt Sylvia and Sam really extended themselves. Then your grandmother was given that enormous birthday cake, and after all the candles were blown, you know she insisted on making a speech."

"A speech?" Abby's laughter rose through the car. "Workers of the World, Unite."

I shook my head, following the road signs as I talked. "She stood up there, surrounded by all of us who had taken time and money to get there, and lamented how hard it was to be alone."

"Oi vey." Abby put out her cigarette, then flipped it

through the window. "But she's not the only one alone. There must have been four or five of you at that table in the same boat."

"That's the point." I nodded again, confused now at the road and the turn-off toward the throughway.

"I think Aunt Sylvia is marvelous," Abby said, "putting up with all of you that way. I always loved her best, you know, of all of them."

"I wonder if we've gone too far."

Abby reached for the sheet of white paper with the directions on it. "Let's see." She followed the little drawing Claude had made down with her finger. "Mmm. The turn-off should be soon. I don't think yet, and it's on the left."

"Let's continue for a mile or two," I said; "if we don't see it, we can turn around."

She lit another cigarette and leaned back. It was on my tongue to note that she was smoking too much. I bit it back. After a mile or so, I pulled the car to the right, off the road. "Let's see the map, shall we?"

She and I fingered it, trying to find the turning. Across the road from us were two truckers, pulled up on their side, outside their cab.

I opened the window and called out to them, my questions floating off in the wind.

"Oh, Mummy," Abby said impatiently. "They can't hear you."

Up ahead I saw the sign of a Total station. I turned to tell her we could ask up there, when I saw she was not in the car.

"What in hell!" I thought. I looked across the road and saw her, map in hand, talking to the truckers. The three of

them looked at the map together and all I could think of
was, "What a dumb thing to do, to cross that road!"

She waved to me triumphantly. "Everything's in order,"
she called, making a round signal O with her fingers.

I turned away to lean to the right side to open the door
for her when I heard a strange noise. I turned and saw a
flight through the air, an arc of bright blue and white. For
an instant, it meant nothing and then I thought, "My God,
it's Abby. Oh, my God." That blue, that Gauloise blue, that
white, the long hair streaming behind in the wind. "It's
Abby, it's Abby."

I leaped out of the car and started to run toward where
she lay, way up the road. Then I turned back. I had left the
car door open. I ran back for my purse; all I could think of
was my passport, my money, Abby. I ran back down the
road, shouting, "No, No, No."

When I came to where she lay on the ground, I think I
knew at once she was dead.

Someone had leaped from another car and was holding
her head, pulling out her tongue. "Go away. Don't touch,"
she said sharply to me.

I edged back and I stood there. I stood looking. "Maybe,"
I thought in a numb, icy dread, "it's for the best, my dearest,
my darling Abby. No more worry. No more pain." Then the
monstrosity of the thought shook me. "Oh, my God. What
am I thinking? What am I thinking!"

I clutched my pocketbook. I began to scream. "Please get
the gendarmes. An ambulance. Please." I knew she was
dead, instantly dead, but might not the doctors save her, I
saw the man whose car had struck Abby. He was young and
terrified and there was blood on his throat. He must have
leaned over her, been spattered.

"You were driving too fast," I said to him quietly, as if I were admonishing him for being late to school.

"It wasn't my fault," he said, his eyes round with terror. "It wasn't my fault."

"You were driving too fast. You shouldn't drive so fast."

I looked at Abby again. The blood was streaming through her hair.

"I'll have to wash it with that shampoo she likes so much," I thought.

I looked at her blue legs; one was cracked, with the bone showing through the blue knit of her stocking. "That won't be hard to set," I thought. "I'll take her back to Connecticut with me. She'll get well there. Or maybe I'll stay here, in Avallon, near the hospital. Then we'll take our trip."

A man ran over to me with one of her blue suede wedge shoes. It had come off her in flight. I took it in my hand and held it, dazed. "I found it," he said. "It was on the road."

"Thank you. Thank you very much." I stared at the shoe blindly. I looked at him, unseeing. Her shoe. So little time between life and death.

He looked at me and backed away. Someone edged me back to the side of the road. "The gendarmes, the ambulance," I kept repeating. "Where are they, why don't they come?"

There was the sound of the siren, breathing in and out, that awful wail of the siren. Then the firemen with their ambulance, two cars of gendarmes, doctors in another car. All the panoply of the auto crash, the crowds, the stalled traffic, the flashing lights above the ambulance. There was the rush for oxygen, for blood transfusions, all of the ritual of modern salvation.

I stood watching. I thought, "I cannot bear it."

"That's Madame, her mother," someone pointed me out.

The doctor approached me. "You can ride in the ambulance back to Avallon with your daughter, madame," he said. The woman who had been administering first aid approached me.

"Thank you, thank you," I said to her. "I hope they'll do their best."

A man standing next to me said, "They'll do the maximum, don't worry."

"Good." I looked at him approvingly. "Oh, good."

But the young woman, the first-aid woman, put her hand on my shoulder. "The maximum may not be enough," she said briskly. "You must face that fact."

"You mean, she may die."

She nodded. "Yes. You must face that."

"Oh, no," I said, "oh, no."

"Yes, but yes," said the woman.

"No," I said.

"Yes."

But I knew she was dead. I had known it at once. The doctor came to me and said, "You'll ride to the hospital with me, in my car."

"But the ambulance? I was told to ride in the ambulance." I hesitated. He pushed me toward his car. I saw them lift Abby on a stretcher and cover her face with a blanket. I knew precisely what that meant, but as I got into the car with the doctor I said, "They'll do the maximum, won't they. They'll do the maximum. That's my Abby."

# 8

The doctor in charge at the hospital was a big, stout, moon-faced, courteous man. "No," he said at once in answer to my question. "No, you cannot go back to Paris tonight. I don't think so. Please stay here. As our guest, won't you?"

I wanted to get back into the car and drive back to Paris and—what was I thinking of: start all over again? I nodded to the doctor, mumbled that he was so kind.

"We'll give you a sedative. You must stay with us."

"Do all you can for Abby, won't you? Do all you can."

He put his arm around my shoulder. I was sitting on a chair in the emergency room. "Madame, please be assured. There is no more to do. She is dead."

I sat there. I wasn't numb. I listened to him. Again he put his arm around my shoulder.

"Your husband, can we notify him?"

"Husband? My husband is newly dead. I am a new widow."

His hand on my shoulder tightened. "Have you other children? Anyone here in France? Is there anyone to notify?"

I bristled at him and answered curtly. "I have two other children. Yes, I have. But what difference does that make? One does not replace the other."

He drew back, his hand on his chest, protesting. "But, madame, I am not trying to pry. I only want to help. You need someone here with you."

"Why? There is nothing to do." I shook my head. I could not take it all in. "What is there to do now? Why disturb anyone else?"

I wanted to disappear. To vanish. To dissolve. This kindly man was talking to me of connective links, of life, of the need for decisions. But I had nothing to decide. The decisions had been made. I wanted to run. I stared at him. Finally I managed to say, "I can't stay here, Doctor. I must call my daughter, my son. I have to get to Paris to telephone them."

"Where can you reach them? Perhaps we can help."

"One is in Ottawa, the other in California. I have to get to Paris to phone."

"Madame," he said, putting his large hand over both of mine, which lay clenched on my knees, intertwined and tight. "Let me assure you, madame, we have telephones in Avallon. Be our guest. I don't want to insist, but I can't let you drive to Paris tonight. We'll put you in your own room and connect a telephone there and you can make all the calls you wish."

A nurse came in and shot me full of a sedative and I was taken to a clean, narrow, white-washed room with two beds in it against the long wall. Both were empty. I sat down in the little chair by the window. What was I going to do? I didn't know what to do. The nurse and a helper, a broad, efficient woman in a cotton print house dress, came in with a telephone that they jacked into a switch beside my chair.

"Something to eat?" said the woman. "The doctor said to bring you something." I shook my head. "No, no thank you."

"Yes," she answered, "the doctor said to get you something. It's past suppertime now, but I can make you a tisane."

I continued to shake my head, even as she left the room to fetch me something. I stared at the telephone at my elbow. "Maybe I won't telephone," I thought. "Maybe it's better not to let anyone know."

The nurse came back. "Will you phone now? The operator has been informed you will be making foreign calls. She's all ready for you."

I stared at the nurse. "Why wasn't she looking?" I asked the young, sweet-faced woman, "What made her run across the road? How could she do a stupid thing like that?" I put my head in my hands. "I'm angry with her. I'm really angry. How could she do it?"

The little nurse put her hand on my arm. Her eyes were wet with tears. "Madame, please. Try to be quiet. Make your calls. Then you can rest."

"But don't you understand? I'm angry. I always tried to make her watch the road. She was always so careless. She couldn't learn to drive."

"It happens, madame. It happens. We see it often. It is always so sad."

Death by auto. I stared at the nurse. Of course. The most ordinary statistic of our time. Auto crash. Death by our own making. Death by carelessness. Terrible, violent, instant death. I could hear again the ping of the body against the car. The shriek of the sirens. The jam in the road. Cars stopped to watch. The crowds. The curiosity. The ambulance with its in-and-out horn, the gendarmes polite, precise. The look in all the eyes, everyone's eyes—it strikes again. Death by auto. So quickly done. So quickly over. One minute laughter. And then silence.

But Abby wasn't a statistic. She was my Abby.

"After the first death," the words of Dylan Thomas flashed through my mind, "there is no other."

"No, no," I said to the nurse, who could only try to comfort me by the tears in her eyes. "It isn't true. Each death has a right to its own identity, its own unique terribleness."

The nurse stroked my arm and then held the telephone toward me, coaxing me to take it, like a sip of medicine. I looked at her blankly, then reached for my handbag. I was beginning to feel the palpable, numbing rise of the sedative, my lips seemed thick and swollen, my fingers stiff. I could not find my address book. I must have neglected to take it. My mind was still clear enough for me to realize that, without the telephone numbers, it would be difficult to place the calls. The information service in France was disastrous. I thought of Abby's bag and her address book.

"Please," I said to the nurse. "I forgot my notebook. I need my daughter's pocketbook. There's a book inside it. Where is it?"

She thought for a moment. "The gendarmes have probably impounded the car. If it's in the car, they will bring it to you."

I sat in the dark while she went out to call the police station. The woman in the printed house dress brought in the tisane in a low, round bowl. She made me get up and sit at the little table, where she placed it. I tried to drink it. It was lukewarm and smelled of peppermint. She watched as I sipped it, and when I said, "No more, please, no more," she leaned over and embraced me.

"It is hard, madame. I know. The hardest of all sorrows for a mother."

I stared at her. She was kind, but sorrow? My sorrow hadn't even begun. It lay there in the shadows ahead of me. I knew it was there, lurking there, an infinite loss, an intolerable pain. But for now, I was hollow, uninhabited. I must telephone. Perhaps someone would tell me what I had to do next.

The nurse returned, followed by a tall young gendarme carrying Abby's straw bag. It looked like her. I stared at it as he handed it to me, then put it on my lap. When he and the nurse left the room, I sat with the bag and thought, "I can't open it. It belongs to her. It's private."

There were desk drawers and closets at home still untouched because I couldn't bear to go through Charles's papers. A university had asked for all his manuscripts and letters and journals and I had agreed, but I was still unable to approach this invasion of his privacy, this intrusion of the living on the dead. His wallet had been at the hospital when he died and I brought it home with me. It didn't seem impertinent to open that—to take out the seven dollars and to see that there was only one photograph in it, a silly picture of Abby at the age of thirteen, taken in one of the Photomaton places at the five-and-ten on Eighty-sixth Street. I remembered fingering that little photo and thinking "I must tell Abby." He had been carrying it for almost twenty years. I had never told her. It had always slipped my mind.

I started to fumble in her little handbag; it was so pretty, so pert, little and efficient. That bag with the pink-red rose

embroidered on it! Was it still there in the shop, waiting for
me to make up my mind? My fingers reached to the bottom
of the bag and came up with her address book. I opened it.
Everything in it was neatly tabulated. It was so like her.
That sense of order beneath the reckless exterior. I noted
the precise, workmanlike handwriting, a block-letter style
she had created for herself. Every address and telephone
number in place—from her grandmother to the notary who
had arranged the purchase of her studio.

I flipped through it. Debby. John. A friend of mine in
Paris. Suddenly I saw Jean's name. I must call him, too, I
thought. How can I not? I lifted the receiver and gave the
operator my numbers: the Ottawa number, the California
number, Jean's number, and the Paris number of my friend.
It didn't matter in what order, I assured the operator,
whichever she arrived at first.

I put down the telephone to wait. It would all take time. I
opened the straw bag to put the little address book back in,
when I picked up her wallet. I held it for a moment, thinking, "I know what I'll find." And I did. The only photograph
in it was of her father—an old photograph, he was in air
force uniform, very young, very dashing, and signed across
the top "to Debby and Abby from Daddy." I tucked the
photograph back in its pocket and sat in the darkened room,
not so much locked in thought, as locked. Shuttered. Sedated.

The woman in the print dress came in to see how I was.
"I'm all right," I assured her. "Don't worry."

"The chief doctor said I was to be in and out"; she
sounded apologetic. "He wanted me to keep watch."

I looked at her vacantly. "Of course," I said. "How good
you all are!"

What did they expect I would do? I was so doped up by

now that my vision was blurred. If there was weeping and despair in my future, it lay behind that narcotic film that wrapped me in. I could hardly do anything to myself, if that's what they were concerned about. I could barely stand to walk across the room.

When the telephone rang, it was Christopher in Ottawa. I was glad it was the first call to go through. I told him very bluntly, very briskly, "Chris, my darling. Abby was killed in an accident on the road this afternoon in Avallon."

"My God," he said, "what are you saying?"

Then I said—unbelievable, but I said it—as I had thought it on the road: "Chris, Chris dear. Maybe it's for the best. She was killed instantly. Do you think it's for the best? She'll never have to suffer again." And then, even as I said it, drugged as I was, I was struck by the enormity of that thought. Best for whom? Best in what way? Was it I who would never have to worry again—about the possibilities of her pain, the possibilities of her back worsening? the possibilities of failure in her work? failure in love? But what of the possibilities of her life, her vast unused talent, she who was at the peak of her beauty, her creative strength, loving and loved? What was I saying?

Suddenly I was so struck by the magnitude of the loss to me, personally to me, I could barely speak.

"Debby is not here," Chris was saying. "Oh, darling, she'll call the minute she comes in. I'll tell her. Are you all right?"

I assured him I was and hung up the telephone, stunned by the simplicity of the conversation. That's all there was to say. Abby is dead.

The telephone rang again and it was Debby. "Oh, Mummy," she said, "say it isn't true, please say it isn't true. We were going to grow old together, we had a plan."

"What did you say?" I asked. "I can't hear you, darling."

But I did hear. She and Abby had always laughed about their plans for growing old together. They had counted on one another. What scrunchy, grunchy, wonderful old ladies they would have been together, I thought. I could not speak.

"Do you hear me, Mother? Are you there? Do you want me to come, Mother?" she shouted on the phone. "I'll come if you want me."

My voice returned. "I hear you, darling. There is no need. I don't know what there is to do. It's all done. I'll have to see."

"But don't you need me?" There was in her voice a passionate and desolate urgency. "Can't I help?"

I tried to think quickly, in practical terms. She had just returned to Canada from London, not five days before. A flight to Europe now, at the height of the season, was expensive. She had her work to prepare for the coming semester. I thought, to spare her I would manage alone.

"I think I can manage," I said. "Honestly I do. I'll let you know if I can't." I was so blurred, I hardly knew what I was saying. I wanted to sleep. I tried to make sense to Debby. "Telephone whomever you think should know at once. I'll speak to you when I get to Paris. But don't call John. I have a call in to him. I want to tell him myself."

We hung up, my click of the receiver cutting off the soft sobbing I could hear at the other end.

But I was counting on Abby too, I thought, when I grew older. I was counting on her loveliness, her understanding, her friendship. I've always counted on it. Abby was important to me. "Don't you realize that," I said to the four walls, "she was important to me."

The telephone rang again and it was Debby once more.

"Mother." She spoke firmly. "I'm coming, whether you

want me or not. I've just made reservations. I'll be at Roissy tomorrow night at twelve-thirty."

Dearest Debby, I thought, wiser than I was about myself.

"Debby, I'm glad. But who will meet you? I don't know where I'll be."

"Don't worry. I'll go to the apartment, and if I can't get in, to a hotel for the night. I'll arrange something. I just want you to know."

"Debby, I love you."

"I know, Mother. And I love you, too."

I sat trembling as we rang off. I called the operator and urged her to try my Paris number next. She did, and my old friend was on the wire. I told her what had happened and asked if she would pick up Debby at Roissy the next night.

"No, no," she protested. "You're more important this minute than she. We'll drive down to Avallon tomorrow afternoon and pick you up to drive you back to Paris. Debby will manage to find her way."

No one was listening to me, I thought. Everything is happening outside me. I sat clutching the telephone on my lap, thinking, "What do I do next?" I jumped when it rang. A man's voice. He wanted to know who was calling him. The operator intervened. "Here is your call, madame," she said. My mind didn't focus. I thought it was a wrong number. I asked the caller why he was calling.

"But you called me, madame." There was an ironic lilt to his voice.

Then I realized. I had put through a call to Jean.

"Jean?" I asked. "Is this Jean?"

"Yes," he answered; his voice was slow, low, resonant.

"Jean, this is Madame Gorham, Abigail's mother."

"Ah, yes," he said. "You are in Burgundy together, aren't you? How are you?"

"Jean," I said, cutting his politeness short. "Jean, I have something terrible to tell you. Abigail was killed on the road this afternoon. She's dead."

There was a momentary silence. "What did you say?"

"I said that Abby is dead. She was killed in an automobile accident this afternoon around five o'clock."

Again silence, and then I heard him crying, calling, "Oh, no, oh, no, oh, no." He wept on the telephone, and I thought if I weren't so drugged, I would weep with him. Finally he said, "Where are you? Are you hurt? Are you all right?"

"I'm in the hospital at Avallon," I said. "But there's nothing the matter with me. The doctor wanted me here the night, to quiet me down. But I'm perfectly all right. I wasn't hurt."

"I'll come at once," he said.

"No, no. There is no need."

"I'll come." He sounded firm.

"At least wait until morning."

"All right, I'll be there in the morning." There was a pause, a frightened pause. "I don't want to see her. I won't be able to see her."

"No," I said. "There is no need."

The phone rang a few more times, beloved Lucy and Marilyn from Connecticut, my brother, those whom Debby had alerted. I fell asleep, barely aware that the nurse undressed me and guided me to the bed.

"I haven't heard yet from my son," I managed to say.

"Never mind." She tucked me in. "Sleep, madame. I'll wake you when he calls."

It was three in the morning before his call came through.

All I can remember of that call were John's words when I told him, his baffled tone as he said, "But she was my childhood."

The next morning, I sat waiting for Jean. I had managed to wash and dress. The drug continued to work even as I awakened, and its effects were still on me. I had no idea of what was now expected of me. There had been an accident. Weren't there formalities to be observed? What were they? Maybe Jean would know. Suddenly I regretted that he was coming. Maybe he would decide not to come after all. Abby had wanted this meeting postponed, deferred, avoided, evaded. I felt somehow as if this might be against her wishes, even behind her back.

But she lay dead now, somewhere in this hospital, and she was his, too—his sorrow, his love. Like the pocketbook that was rifled, the wallet poked into, like the address book that was examined, the living decided for the dead what was private and what was not.

I was tired, empty, quite wooden by now. I had slept after talking with John in California and awakened with the light that splattered through the tall bare window like shattered glass. It was hot and clammy. The nurse had helped me out of the hospital gown and back into my T-shirt and slacks. She had washed my face with a hot cloth, had combed my hair. She was careful and tender. I couldn't quite remember why I was here, nor account for her solicitude. The same tall, round-faced doctor of yesterday came in and asked me how I was.

I said to him, some game I was playing, "You are sure my daughter is dead."

"Yes, madame," he answered quietly, gravely. "Quite sure,

madame." He looked at me closely. "Is there someone to be with you? Someone to take you back to Paris?"

I nodded. "Yes. American friends. They will be here about four."

He came over to me, put his hand on my shoulder. "Good," he said. "I'm glad you have someone. Good-by, madame. Take care of yourself. Good-by."

After he left, I sat. Waiting. When Jean came in, I stared at him. I had forgotten he was coming. But I knew him at once. I went to the open door to meet him. We embraced and clung silently.

"I don't want to see her," he said. "Never this way." He was trembling.

"I know. It doesn't matter. Do as you wish."

"Have you been down?"

"No." I, too, began to tremble, shaking so I clutched my arms to my side. "No. I should. But I can't. I saw her on the road."

"We'll go back to Paris as quickly as possible, yes? Where is the car? We must make arrangements."

"The gendarmes have the car." I was still shaking. "Arrangements?" Oh, God, of course. My trembling and shaking were almost uncontrollable. Arrangements! It was true, wasn't it? It was true.

Jean led me back to the chair at the window. "I'll be back. Then we'll go."

I remembered. "But I have friends driving down to get me. They will be here at four."

He looked at me, shook his head. "No. Try to reach them. Or leave them a note. You shouldn't stay here until four."

He left the room then and was gone for a long time. When he returned, he had the keys to the rented car. "The gendarmes will be here soon. You must sign a report. Then the undertaker," he stumbled over the word. "You have to decide what you want done."

Decide? Of course. "Cremation," I said. "I have no religious feeling about it. Tell them cremation."

His face, pink-cheeked and round, seemed young and afraid, so young beneath the unexpected aureole of silver hair that curled in a mop around his head. His eyes were very blue, the same blue as the blue-jean jacket he wore. They darkened in pain and panic at the word cremation. I felt his uncertainty.

"If you prefer otherwise, Jean, we'll do it your way."

"No, no," he said. "You are quite right. It is for you to decide. Whatever you say."

I really didn't care. I had no feeling. Death was the end. Everything else was annotation.

The police arrived, two of them, lean and tall and crisp. We shooks hands all around; it was like a French reception. Then they listened to my statement, given under the prod of their questions. When I said I would not prefer criminal charges against the driver of the car that had mowed Abby down, all three Frenchmen, Jean and they, seemed relieved. They knew how punitive such a charge could be.

"She was on the road, running across it, she had no right to be there," I said flatly, so tired I could hardly manage the words. "He isn't criminal, that young man. He was going too fast. I want him charged with that. Nothing more."

Then the police left, and the undertaker arrived. A fat, jolly man wearing a checkered sweater vest over his open brown shirt. A storekeeper kind of man, without any trace of the *pompes funèbres*. His face clouded too when I said cremation. That meant Père-Lachaise, in Paris, he explained.

But if that was what was wanted, he would see to it. I confirmed this and the matter was arranged.

"As quickly as possible," I stressed.

"These things take time," he said. "We must convey the body. There are papers."

Jean cut him short. "As quickly as possible. I'll arrange for the papers." We all shook hands. It seemed odd and vaguely sociable. And then we were ready to go.

Jean and I went down to the first floor and I headed for the office. But Jean took my arm and steered me away.

"Let's go down the stairs," he said. He led me to the basement below. There was a small chapel there with wooden benches, and behind the little altar was a wooden partition.

"Abigail is there," he said, "behind the partition."

There? "How do you know?" I asked. "Who told you?"

"I came down here before," he said. "I asked." That's why he had been gone so long.

There were candles burning on the little altar, and flowers in a basket. I sat on one of the wooden benches and thought, "Our Father Who art in heaven," because it was all I could think of thinking. We stayed a few minutes and left. I paid my bill at the office, and then we drove back to Paris in almost complete silence, leaving the candles and the wooden wall and Our Father behind.

Only as we neared the city outskirts did I know that I was back from our trip to Burgundy. I looked out the car window and saw a flight of birds rising quickly from a tired and dusty plane tree alongside the incoming boulevard. Their flight, the lift into the air, caught at my throat.

"Oh, Abby, my darling, are you out there somewhere or entirely inside me?" I asked. The sky was like pale watered silk, like gray moire, soft to the touch of the eye, and I saw the birds disappear into its folds.

Jean drove me to Marie-Claude's apartment. It was all closed up, as I had left it the day before. I opened the windows, let in the noise and air and clamor from the street.

"Why don't you rest," Jean suggested. "I have something I must do. I'll be back. We'll have something to eat and I'll drive you to Roissy to pick up Debby."

"Will you? Oh, I'm so glad," I said.

His tone was calm, matter-of-fact. "But of course. I'll be back. We'll have to go in your car." He had come to Avallon by train so he could drive the rented car to Paris. "Mine is in the country. We can have a bite somewhere in an hour or two, when I come back. You sleep."

I slept as if in a fever. How could the impossible be possible? How could I accept the unacceptable? What I had always feared would happen, had happened. Why? Flight. The blue and white above me. Over and over again. Flight. The blue and white. I awoke, drenched in sweat, to the sound of the doorbell.

Jean and I ate somewhere, then drove to the airport. We arrived a bit early and sat silently, waiting. The place was almost empty, it was midnight, the wide white corridors stretching on all sides in a stark, minimalist perspective. Suddenly a gay young group, a family group—two young women, a young man, and a young child—seated themselves on the benches next to us. The child ran out and captured a luggage cart that stood at the door and started wheeling it back and forth in front of us. I stared at the little girl as she gyrated around the wire wagon. The young mother thought I looked disapproving and called to the child, "Stop fooling with the chariot, Mimi, stay quiet."

I managed a wan smile at the mother that it didn't matter, that I was not being disturbed. That same instant, first off the New York plane, came the sister or friend for whom they were waiting, a breathless, happy teen-ager carrying an armful of packages which she thrust at them; a chorus of joyous greetings. There was a big plastic bag of M&M chocolates which she threw to the young mother.

"M&M's!" shrieked the mother; "what a wonderful gift! I adore them."

The child jabbed at her mother. "What are they? what are they?"

Her mother tucked the bag of candy under her jacket. "Not for children," she said; "these are medicaments. Dangerous for children," and they all broke into wild laughter as we saw Debby approach. We stood, the three of us, holding one another, clutching one another, as the laughter rang through the empty corridors.

Jean stayed at the apartment that night, sleeping on the living-room couch, while Debby and I shared the bed. The next morning was hot again, muggy. The ash tray in front of the couch was laden with butts. Jean must have smoked through the night. We found some crusts of bread in the refrigerator, some coffee. We took turns using the bathroom to wash and dress. We faced going to Abby's studio, calling her friends, packing her things—arrangements, arrangements.

The studio was cool and austere. The paintings on the wall blazed with color, in their own bright austerity. We stared at the paintings—at the unfinished one on the easel that awaited the yellow background on her return. It was unbearable. There was the sharp awareness not only of tremendous personal loss but of that other loss—the wider flights that would never be made, the superb skill that would remain unrealized to its fullest.

"A painter needs a long life," I said. "She said it herself. She was just at a turning point."

Debby came and put her arms around me. "She did so much in her short life, Mother. So very much. You must remember that. Look around." She circled the room. "See," she waved her hand around the walls and then pointed to the portfolios stacked against the drawing board. "The paintings, the drawings, the water colors." Again she held me close. "You must remember, in so many ways Abby was lucky. She was living exactly the life she wanted. She died at a moment when her life was absolutely her own, on her own terms."

I clung to her. "It's the suddenness, Debby. The terrible, terrifying suddenness. I can't absorb it." I wanted to wail. To tear my hair. I held onto her.

She tightened her hold. "I know. It's so hard to accept the fragility of the human body. We're built like birds. All that heart and soul on such a frail, spindly bone structure, that can be crushed like a bird's—like that."

Jean stood in the center of the room, stunned, overwhelmed by the return to this place. "I'm going out," he said. "I'll buy some food. I'll bring it back. I won't be long." He fled.

We began to empty the closets, to stack the clothes. Everything was clean, neatly folded, as if ready for inspection, orderly.

I tried to joke. "I would hate anyone to go through my closets," I said. "I'm neat on the surface. Not like this. Look how Abby kept everything," and then I burst into tears.

"Sit down, Mother; I'll do it." Debby tried to lead me to the bed.

"No, it has to be done. We'll do it together."

Everything else in the studio was as precisely organized as the clothes. The unpaid bills were neatly stacked. They had been unpaid for years, I noted, but they were clearly organized. A blue portfolio on which she had lettered the word DOCUMENTS was tucked into a drawer. In it was all the information on the purchase of the apartment, the name of the notary, the name of the agent. Her paint tubes were laid out carefully, her brushes clean beside her easel. On her drawing board were her pencils, T-square, ruler, each in position—the position she had given them. By their side was a notebook. It was an artist's notebook. Filled with ideas on painting, clear definitions of her conceptions of the paintings on the wall, proposals for future paintings, ideas on life and art. She had been so pretty, sometimes so diffident, so funny and so gay and often so humble, that it was easy to forget her profundity. Debby and I read the notebook together and it wounded us in the same way. It was so Abby. So expectedly, so unexpectedly Abby.

I thought of her at the pine table, alone in the evening, afire with ideas, with her whole world there within her, dealing with her sensations, her perceptions, her soaring spirit, recording it all with articulate precision. Abby getting down to her marrow, shedding her skin. Abby lit from within by her own, unborrowed, sentient intelligence.

I closed the notebook and sat on the bed with my head in my hands. "It is so unfinished, so unfinished."

Debby stood with her hand on the notebook, her face stiff with pain. "She had so many pictures to paint," she said, "so much love to love, so much laughter to laugh. Oh, Mother!"

I looked at her, and suddenly her living sorrow—she was alive, she was my Debby—clutched at me. I got off the bed and went and put my arms around her.

"Let's try to finish packing, darling. Even if I don't know quite what we're doing."

"Yes," she agreed softly.

I turned toward the books, the records. "But what do we do with it all? What are we packing for? Where does it go?"

Debby walked over to the shelf of toy soldiers. She touched them gently. "She has always had these. If you don't mind, Mother, I'd love to take them."

I shook my head. "Take anything, anything. I haven't the faintest notion what we do now."

Debby put her arms around me again. "Why don't we leave things for now? Jean and I will buy a trunk. We'll manage."

Jean? He had been gone a long time.

"I wouldn't blame him," Debby said, "if he didn't come back, poor guy"; she shook her head; "if he just disappeared."

I nodded.

"It's worse for him," she went on, "much worse. She was his daily life for so long."

When Jean did come back, he was red-eyed and tired-looking. "I went to see Jacques. I told him. We must tell her friends. She had so many. Some are away now, it's August. But we must let them know."

There was no food. Jean had forgotten to bring it. So I went down to the Rue Didot and brought back some cheese, bread, and tomatoes. We sat and ate silently, the window open on the balcony, the breeze filtering through the green plants that Abby had hung above the ledge.

"I also called the undertaker at Père-Lachaise," Jean broke the silence. "They'll try to arrange it for Tuesday. I have to go see him this afternoon to complete the details."

Jean knew that Debby wanted to get back to Ottawa and the university as quickly as possible. He knew I was on the edge of personal crisis. He was trying to speed things up. He had taken over all the grim, necessary paperwork that Debby and I didn't even know had to be done. He was making all the telephone calls from the corner café, trying to ferret through the French network of documents, official releases, and rubber stamps.

"We'll go with you to Père-Lachaise," I said. "There's no reason for you to go alone."

We traveled to the east of Paris, to the buildings where such things are arranged. Unlike the jolly storekeeper undertaker in Avallon, with his checkered vest and open shirt, the man here wore the stiff, formal costume of his trade. He was businesslike and brisk. He warned us of complications.

"The papers must come from Auxerre; that's where they must be signed," he said, "before we can proceed. And the mails are very undependable. I cannot confirm Tuesday for cremation. And if it isn't Tuesday, we have no opening until Friday afternoon."

I became very agitated, my disturbance showed, I shook with cold in the air-conditioned room.

Jean looked at Debby and saw the dismay on her face. He turned to the bureau official. "No," he said brusquely, "it must be Tuesday. I will go to Auxerre myself to pick up the papers to make certain they are here on time."

The man in charge of our "case" seemed irritated. He stroked his mustaches carefully, neatly, not getting them out of place.

"But it's *our* job to make certain the papers arrive," he announced.

"Surely," said Jean, "you don't mind if I help expedite it. I'll drive down myself. If I pick up the papers and bring them back, then can you guarantee it?"

The young man shrugged. "Yes, if you'll do that. But," again he was very practical, clinging to his procedure, "that's part of *our* job. We're supposed to arrange about the papers. We can't make any reductions in the price if you do it."

Jean made an impatient gesture. "No, no. I understand. The price is the price. But we can't wait too long. I'll go myself."

As we were driving back toward the south of Paris, I remembered the word price. I turned to Jean. "That man said he gave you a price, Jean. What was it?"

He tried to brush it aside.

"I insist," I said. "I can't have you take over the expenses."

He looked at me quietly, his blue eyes very intense, weighing the matter. "Okay," he said. "We'll go half and half. But you must let me and I'll let you." We agreed.

On the way back, we stopped, and Debby and Jean went out to buy a trunk while I sat in the car waiting. I was worn out, exhausted. I was relieved they were there to take over.

When we were back at the studio, Debby and Jean carried the trunk upstairs. It looked like a green coffin, and I sat shivering on the bed as I looked at it. The two of them stared at me.

"Is it all right?" Jean asked.

"It's what we could find," said Debby.

My silly trembling. I couldn't stop it. Jean looked at me.

His eyes narrowed. "You don't like the way it looks?" he asked.

I nodded.

"I know," he said. He went over to Abby's worktable, got some brushes and acrylic paint, yellow and white and blue, and painted some squiggly lines, some gay blobs over the top and sides. I stopped shivering and looked at him gratefully.

There was a knock at the door. It was Roy, a friend of Abby's, an artist whose atelier was around the corner. Abby had been very fond of him. He came in now and sat with us, looked at the gaily painted trunk and around the room.

"This place is just like her. It is an environment all its own. Everything about it. Everything in place, composed, simple, superb. You must never change it. Keep it that way, just that way." Again his eyes settled on the trunk.

"She hated anything out of order. The trunk is out of place," I said, following his eyes.

Roy nodded. "She was so in order herself. Her life was an art. She was an art. Such a lovely woman." His sand-colored hair and beard seemed to quiver as he puffed on his pipe, lighting it continually, speaking slowly. "Unless you need the money desperately, why should you give up this studio? Why not keep it? At least for now."

Of course, I thought. That's the answer. Why make the decisions now? Why pack? What's the rush? "I think you're right," I decided suddenly. "I think I'll wait. I'll wait and see."

Debby reached over and took my hand. "That's good. It's all too fast. How do we know how we'll feel next year? And there's always David."

I squeezed Debby's hand. David, my grandson David.

"When I grow up," he had said to me that very summer, right before I came to Europe, "I'd love an apartment just like Aunt Abbo's." What if it seemed wasteful, extravagant? I would think that out later.

After Roy left, I asked Jean if he didn't want to take over the studio for the time being. "No, no"; he shook his head vehemently. "I have my own studio. This was her place. It was always her place. I could never stay here, never."

The news of Abby's death had spread. Some other friends came, shocked and desolate, not believing, grieving. One friend offered us his apartment, which had a telephone, if there were calls to be made. The offer was welcome. We went with him to his place on a street behind the Boulevard Pasteur. He was the director of a film animation studio, and the telephone was in the room with his drawing boards and desk. It made an odd, modern, workmanlike clutter against the huge Second Empire furniture that jostled it. The heavy polished walnut pieces were everywhere—handsome, solid, archaic. I remarked at their period beauty.

"I was born here," said he, "these were my parents'; this was their apartment."

Yes, I thought, this is the way it is in Paris. Generation after generation in one apartment. My aunt and her family had lived in theirs, in Belleville, for more than fifty years.

"I may never myself go back to France," I thought; "I may never be able to be in Paris again, but somehow, in some way, why shouldn't Abby's studio follow its own Parisian pattern, a permanent place for bits and pieces of her family, too?"

I wasn't clear about it. Perhaps it sprang from a reluctance to do anything decisive at once. But when we returned from our many telephone calls, I confirmed my decision.

"We'll keep the place," I said. "There's no reason not to. I didn't count on this money. It was Abby's, given to her. I feel better, knowing the place will be here."

Jean drove Debby and me to the apartment in Montparnasse that night and departed with the promise to pick us up the next morning at ten. We had eaten a sketchy dinner, and we sat, sipping some of the house vermouth, terribly tired but unable to face the sleepless night ahead.

It was the first we had been alone since her arrival. I felt how bone-tired she must be, with no time to recover from the inevitable jet lag, the immediate plunge into the depths of our grief, as well as the myriad problems of disposal.

I reached over to take her hand. She looked up at me, beneath the curved fringe of her hair, her eyes swollen with tears. "I want you to know how glad I am that you are here, Debby. That you came."

Debby pressed my hand tightly. "You don't always make clear how you feel, Mother. I was afraid you didn't want me. But I had to come."

"I wanted you, darling. I just didn't want to make it tough for you. All that money, the time, it's a bad time for you to be away."

"This kind of thing always comes at a bad time, doesn't it?" She looked at the drink, sipped it. "It's so unbearable. It's so awful."

I nodded. "Awful. It's so unnatural. So unnatural. Children aren't supposed to die before their parents. I can't absorb it."

She stroked my hand. "Mother, please," she tried to comfort me. "As a matter of fact, a century ago a woman had ten children, twelve, fourteen, and she was lucky if three survived. Death is terribly, terribly natural at any time."

I thought for a moment, decided to say what was on my mind although it sounded screwy. "I want to tell you something I've been thinking. I can't get it out of my head. I feel somehow as if this is one death, the same death, Abby and Daddy. Somehow, it has happened together."

She drew back and was silent for an instant. "No, it's not the same. They were close." Her eyes closed and the tears came beneath the shuttered lids. "They were very close. They loved each other very much. Daddy was really able to give Abby a father's love." Her face was troubled, solemn. "He never could to me. He treated me as his own father treated him. He was demanding, harsh, quite Victorian. I was supposed to be the best, the brightest. And he had so many mixed reactions with John. But for Abby it was pure and lovely and direct." The tears were heavy on her cheeks now. I felt a crushing cramp in my chest.

The books he had brought her, the long philosophical discussions; I tried feebly to remind her of them now. She brushed my words aside impatiently. "It's all right now, Mother. It really is. I now think of Daddy as a very interesting parent. Not the best father in the world. But interesting and valuable in my life. But for Abby he was the best father in the world, the very best."

It was true. Charles's love toward Abby had been the easiest, the most uncomplicated. And because his love was so freely given to her, it left me the least amount of motherly guilt and the greatest freedom to be myself with her. We could be mother and daughter, not rivals, not claimants. His love for the other two had been thorny, demanding, complicated. Too much asked, too little given, too much

thrust upon them, and I too silent, too compliant. "You always give in to him," Debby had once wailed to me over I
know not what. But it was the heart of the matter.

What a residue of resentment my passivity must have left
in her, my eagerness not to make waves. Abby was able to
value me as she valued her father, because most of the time
we were separate human beings in her life; I didn't have to
be an extension of him. As I embraced Debby now, clinging
to her, I realized that she had had to win her way toward
me, had had to learn to forgive and forget my fears and in-
eptitudes, my cringings and deceptions, as I had had to forgive and forget her antagonisms and passions.

My cheeks were as wet as her own as I kissed her. "It's too
bad some of the ideas of women's liberation weren't around
a generation ago," I tried to joke, wiping my face with my
sleeve. "They could have been useful."

She tried to joke back. "One step at a time, Mother. Or,
rather, two steps forward, one step back. At least you always
worked. You always cared. And I love you dearly. You are so
dear to me now."

"And you, my darling, to me. I love you so deeply. I
value you so much."

We stood close as we said good night.

Jean arrived for us the next morning after breakfast. He
seemed very tentative as he greeted us. Quite odd.
"Wouldn't you like to drive to the country?" he asked. "It
will be better than being in Paris all day."

It seemed an unexpected suggestion, but still, we were
putting in time. We were all edgy. There was so little to do
as we waited for Tuesday. This was Sunday. We agreed. I
went off to turn in the rented car to the garage around the
corner, while Debby raced across the street to the Paris-

Sheraton to make some long-distance calls. We met again at Jean's car, which stood at the curb.

Debby was excited. "John is flying from California," she told me; "he'll be in Ottawa when we arrive. Isn't that great?"

I nodded. I couldn't speak, I felt so grateful. I looked at her to go on.

"He was desolate; he couldn't afford the money to come all the way here. But he'll be in Canada when we return."

Again I nodded and managed to say, "There was no need to come here, but I'm so glad I will see him the minute I return. I'm so glad."

Jean had a look on his face of utter desolation as he stood waiting for us to get in the car. We were Abby's family and we would soon be gone. Something went on for us on the other side of the ocean. I wondered how it would be for him here. "Rough," I thought as I got in the car, "very very rough."

We headed north through the city, up strange avenues, streets I had never seen. We drove through three-story dinginess, that peculiar French ugliness of masonry and cement-block decay—shabby small garage after small garage, the whole motorized civilization disemboweled and spread everywhere to the naked eye. Parts shops, gasoline stands, motor-bike exchanges, used-car lots.

Suddenly Jean leaned over to the tape deck he had behind the glove compartment.

"Do you mind if I play some music?" He looked at me and then turned to Debby sitting in back.

"I don't mind," she said; "no, play." He turned to me again.

"No. I don't mind. It's a good idea."

I was dense with my own grief. I felt nothing but emptiness. No tears, no tension. Simply a vast open soreness, a sense of aching apprehension. Jean snapped in a tape on the machine, started it, and the little car was filled with music.

"Simon and Garfunkel," I said, those familiar voices, that familiar sound. My lips were frozen, almost rigid. He nodded. Simon and Garfunkel here in the dreck end of Paris. That record she had loved so much. She had filled her room with its rosemary and thyme when she was a teen-ager at home. Simon and Garfunkel, Bach and Mozart, Bob Dylan and Joplin. The music never stopped. Suddenly I had a vision of the two of them, Jean and Abby, driving to the country on a week-end morning, surrounded by music, beating time as the car moved, lovely and happy together.

How good of him, I thought, how warm and understanding, trying to let Debby and me know something of their life together—the foolish part, the fun part. I could taste my tears as the song encased me in its sweet nostalgia, with that melancholy and heartache that is the power of remembered popular music. I cried without moving, not even looking for Kleenex, simply cried to the music. When the song ended, Jean snapped in a Dylan tape, and now I could poke at my face, trying to wipe away the salt.

"She loved Dylan," said Debby, "she and John were early Dylan. They played him all the time, knew all the words."

Jean nodded. It was difficult to speak above the speakers in the car—there must have been three of them in that little space. The way Abby would have loved it, drenched in the music, beating time to it, sitting happily within the shimmering bubble it formed around her.

There were so many things out of her growing-up that she never discarded. Blasting out the words to a song, off key, joyously, raucously. A vivid memory came to me: Three of us in an old convertible, Abby and her friend Mary and I, driving back from Provincetown, the two girls singing wildly in the wind to a loud tune on the car radio. The top of the car was down, the summer's evening had a bite to it as we moved swiftly on the highway. I remember turning my head away from the wheel as the two screeched merrily, pounding the car to the rock rhythm that shook it, thinking, "How happy they are; will they ever be this happy again?"

We crossed a long bridge and were out of Paris. Jean swerved sharply right, following a river. The Oise, said the sign. And then so quickly, past the riverbank, we were in the country. Weekend crowds, boating parties, open cafés filled with festive boys and girls, men and women, children. There were strollers everywhere, edging the riverbank, walking along the road single file against a stand of trees. Jean wheeled the car carefully through the crowds, and then again we were on a continuing road for a few more miles and then through a pleasant old town.

Here he pulled the car to the curb in front of a little two-story building with a restaurant at the street level, the Auberge Van Gogh. He leaped out of the car and looked in the window.

"It's closed," he cried out in disappointment. "I wanted to take you here to dinner."

We got out of the car and joined him at the curb. It looked like a charming restaurant, red-checked curtains, an attractive dark-paneled interior. Above the restaurant, on the second story, was a plaque. Van Gogh had lived and died here. I was surprised. Somehow, I had always thought of him merged into Provence, sick there, buried there. But, no, this was the house of his final years.

"Perhaps you should have telephoned the restaurant," said Debby. "It's a pity you made the trip."

"No, no," he protested. "I wanted you to see it anyway. It doesn't matter." He was obviously crestfallen, regretful.

We got back into the car.

"Was this a place you came to often, Jean, with Abby?" I asked.

"Yes," he answered rather abruptly. "Yes. She loved it. It wasn't too far from Paris." He hesitated. "Maybe we should have come more often."

I knew what he meant. His face, so shining and rosy, beautiful beneath that tangle of silver hair, darkened with a sudden spasm of bitterness. It was too late now to go more often. It would never be enough.

We drove up the little main street and turned a bit left. Above, on a rise of the road, there was a statue. We turned and circled a handsome twelfth-century church and then continued up. A painted arrow said CIMETIÈRE, VAN GOGH. Jean backed down away from the cemetery road and we cut around the statue, back toward the main street.

DAUBIGNY, read the plaque on the statue.

"What is the name of this town," I asked. "I didn't know Van Gogh was buried here. And this statue of Daubigny—?"

"It is Auvers. Auvers-sur-Oise. Yes, Van Gogh is here and his brother, too."

We turned back toward Paris. "Perhaps we can eat in one of those pretty restaurants on the river," Debby suggested.

"Yes, all right," he agreed, but his heart wasn't in it. He had wanted us to share Abby's place. He looked close to tears.

It was dark when we returned to Paris. We were exhausted, and the next day, Monday, Jean planned to leave at six in the morning to go to Auxerre for the papers. Debby offered to make the long drive with him and he welcomed it. She felt his loneliness and his need. I, too, thought he should not make that long trip, up and back, alone. But I couldn't make it with them. I hadn't the strength.

I spent the day in a stupor in the apartment, waiting for them. I read, over and over again, how to put on rouge, what to wear at Saint Tropez, all about the new money and the tourist crowds, about another new young French husband helping another new young French wife, and I was sick with fear for the safety of those two on the frantic August roads. When they returned, at three in the afternoon, they picked me up and we rushed to the funeral place to get all the official documents into the proper hands.

As we got out of the car, Jean reminded me. "Remember what we said."

"What?"

He made a gesture crossing his two index fingers. "Half and half."

"Yes. If you want."

"I want."

It was done. We went in. We turned over the papers, which the official sniffed at but had to find in order. We paid. All arranged. Tomorrow, without fail. At two-thirty. Debby and Jean asked if we couldn't have half an hour alone when the body was delivered. The official promised.

The next morning, we bought flowers on the Avenue du Maine and we each carried a bouquet. I wanted white and blue. Jean said, "In France, white flowers are for a child."

"I want them anyway, dear Jean. She was not a child, no, but mine."

We bought wine and crackers and left them at the studio.

Her friends were to meet us there after four. We wanted no one else with us at Père-Lachaise. Just the three of us.

We arrived early so we could park the car and wait for the arrival from Avallon. We told the guards that we had asked for, and gotten, permission to be alone with her and to put our flowers on the box.

"Yes, yes," we were told. "Just wait here. We'll call you when the car arrives."

Debby and I walked hand in hand along the streets of the cemetery, not speaking, clutching our flowers. I had always thought it romantic to wander around the graves of Père-Lachaise. Abby and I had visited Colette's ugly granite headstone once and been broken up with laughter over the cats that suddenly sprang up on the monument, like the ghosts of minet-chéri, of Saha, startling the hell out of us. I wanted to tell Debby about that day, but couldn't. It was different now. The round, Panthéon dome of the Colum-barium, as they called the crematorium, shadowed the walk. It was a massive, scary building, and I had always hated it. Suddenly Jean signaled that we had better get back to it. We stood at the corner, waiting.

There was some kind of mixup at the last minute, and an attendant rushed out to say the body had arrived, we had better hurry. They rushed us down the side entrance into the corridor just as the little pine box was moving on the conveyor belt into the furnace. In desperation, we thrust our flowers on the box. Quickly, all—box, flowers, Abby—disap-peared through the flipping curtain while we wept loudly, in frustration, in anger, in revolt, because we had not been granted our brief request for privacy, that moment alone.

"Damn them," said Debby, "we asked for some time alone. We asked them. We asked them. Damn them."

I was disintegrated. All I could think of was how small the box was. It was clean and simple and scrubbed-looking, the kind of box Abby liked, but so small. I turned to go. it was so quickly over. But there was more confusion. Jean was talking to the attendants. He turned and said to us, "I must stay. It's French law. There must be a witness, not a member of the family."

Debby was distraught. "Why didn't they tell us? We could have arranged for someone. You *are* a member of the family. Can't we hire someone now?"

Jean put his arm around her lovingly. "No, don't worry. I'll take you outside and find a taxi. Then I'll be back here. It takes an hour, they said. I can do it."

Jean, so fearful of cremation, deeply fearful—but there was no one else to bear witness. We passed the other groups outside the Columbarium, waiting their turn at the conveyor belt. It was a busy day.

Jean found a taxi at the corner and gave the driver the directions. "I'll see you later," he said. Maybe I won't come to the studio when everyone is there. I'll come afterward." We kissed good-by.

Debby was shaking with grief and rage. "Damn them. We wanted just a half hour to sit there quietly with her. Why couldn't they have arranged it?"

I held her in the taxi as we crawled through the traffic, the noise, the heat. "Maybe it's better this way," I tried to comfort her. What was there to say? "There are no good-bys in this, are there?"

"Oh, my darling Abby, my dearest Abby," Debby wept. "I can't bear it, Mother. I can't bear it. I can't believe it. It can't be true."

She was quiet by the time we reached the studio at last.

"If Jean doesn't come back to see everyone, we'll have to understand," she said as we got out of the car. It was almost four. Everything inside was serene and ready. We put out glasses, opened the wine. Soon the studio was full of people. Some I had already met on other visits. All I had heard about, knew by name and Abby's estimate of them. Debby, who had been so staunch and calm until this afternoon, was shattered now. There was a young woman, a French-Canadian painter, who embraced Debby like a child, and Debby stood crying on her shoulder while Geneviève rocked her back and forth.

"Where is Jean?" everyone asked.

We explained about the witness, the law. "It was wicked to make him be the witness. It must have been so hard for him to stay," I said.

"But of course," said one young man; "naturally it was he who had to stay."

Everyone spoke in a hushed tone, sipping the wine, formal and suspended. Roy had come in carrying a single long-stemmed rose and one of his own works, inscribed to Abby. It was of stark white plaster, ovoid impressions embedded in the square, a cold deep negativeness, pure and simple. Except for Debby's weeping, there was almost no sound.

Then Coraline, a friend with whom Abby had worked at the film studio, a tender red-headed woman I had met the year before, reached into her purse to show me a photograph she had long carried of Abby. It was Abby laughing, her hair piled on top of her head, a bottle of wine on the table next to her, her eyes enormous with merriment, responsive to someone across the table, anyone, everyone. The picture went the rounds of the room. Suddenly, the hushed tone disappeared. It was as if Abby had walked in, their darling, their own. I had such a sense of the warmth and kinship these people had felt for her. I thought, "How lucky she was, how beautiful these friends, this affection, this understanding!"

Now, in a rush, they were talking about her directly, and then they began talking about her painting, about how she had finally decided to try for a show, and the idea ran around the room that they would get together to arrange a memorial exposition.

We opened one of her portfolios that stood aslant against the wall and out spilled dozens of drawings. We all sat on the floor now, crowding around, admiring, exclaiming. I found another portfolio with old samples from her illustration days in New York.

"But she never told us," they said. "We had no idea she had done all this. She must have made a fortune."

I nodded. "She did. But she thought, why work this hard when somebody else is throwing the money away?"

Geneviève laughed. "But she was right. Why work for someone else to piss it out."

"Anyway," I added, "she was through with this. It wasn't what she wanted."

What she wanted, the beginning of it, was on the walls, in her latest portfolio, in her head and at her fingertips. We were all painfully aware that it was now all there was, but it was what she had wanted. She hadn't put if off. It was here.

The room was full of talk and laughter when Jean arrived. I was momentarily startled to see him. I didn't think he would have the heart to come back. But he was here. He signaled me across the room, and I followed him into the bathroom to talk privately.

He handed me three little rings, Abby's rings. The undertaker had taken them off her fingers and here they were. There was one with two hearts on it that twisted around so it could be made smaller or larger. I gave it to him and he put it on his little finger. There was a second with a tiny square of turquoise on it, which I slipped on mine. The third, I said to Jean, would be for Debby.

"I wanted you to know," he said quietly, "that it's all right now about the cremation. I talked to someone there. He said to me that what happened today is the same as would be in fifty years from now, the same process. Even the Church agrees."

He was reassuring me, reassuring himself. I thought how easy it is if there is no conviction about death and the body. If one believes the body is truly a remnant, a leftover after death, what does it matter how it is disposed of? But what if one had questions, other feelings? How painful this must have been for Jean!

"It's finally all ashes, Jean," I sought to comfort him further, "even the Bible says so."

"I know," he agreed. "It's all right now."

But even as he said it I wondered if it was. Perhaps he should have been firmer, more insistent. I would have accepted a mass and burial. But it was too late.

We went back into the studio. Jean walked across the room to Jacques Vallet, Abby's poet friend, and talked to him in a whisper. They left the room together. It was almost an hour before they returned, and we had run out of wine. But everyone was waiting for their return. It seems they had driven to the house outside of Paris where Jean's mother lived and which had a garden, to bury the box of ashes for safekeeping. Still ahead was the decision of what to do with them.

Jean said to all of us in the studio, "You know that cemetary in Auvers, where Van Gogh is buried?"

Everyone knew. Debby and I knew too, because of our trip on Sunday.

"That's where I want her to be," Jean announced firmly.

"Impossible," said Alix, "a beautiful thought, but impossible. You know the law?"

The law, of course. French law. Burial permitted only in one's own commune.

"Except through special arrangements," Jean persisted. "We'll have to make special arrangements."

Jacques laughed slyly. "I wouldn't mind the special arrangements of doing it ourselves, some good dark midnight."

Jean nodded in agreement. "Maybe. Maybe we'll have to come to that. But perhaps we can make legal special arrangements, somehow."

The next day was Wednesday. We were due to fly to Ottawa on Thursday morning. Jean arrived early Wednesday morning and asked us to come down to his car.

"If you don't mind," he said. "Shall we drive again to Auvers?"

We took the same route through Paris and again the music played, the requiem music that filled the car, jazzy and sweet and elegiac: "he holds his crayon rosary" then "feelin' groovy." When we reached the town, we drove past the Van Gogh house, took the turn to the left beyond the statue of Daubigny, and this time continued up the little hill, past the church, and to the cemetery.

A small, very French cemetery, fronted by a decorative

iron gate. It seemed like an old-fashioned French garden perched on top of a hill, surrounded by open fields. Inside Jean guided Debby and me past the carved marble headstones, the rows of nicely mounded earth, to two flat beds of thick green ivy. VINCENT VAN GOGH. THEODORE VAN GOGH. Small markers above the thick deep mats of green. We looked, then walked around and came out the gates. There was a field facing the cemetery that rolled to the edge of the hill.

"Van Gogh painted that field," said Jean, "his last painting, I think the one with the crows." Suddenly it had the painting's familiarity; it was a welcoming vista. We turned to look back at the iron gates.

"Would this be all right with you here," Jean asked me, "if we could arrange it?"

I ached for him. It seemed so impossible, so sad, so wildly romantic somehow so Victorian. "*I weep for Adonais—he is dead.*"

"Jean," I touched his arm lovingly, "you know how I feel. It would be right for me if we could strew her ashes over the Loire or the Oise right here, or anywhere she loved. I agree that what remains should remain in France; I don't intend to take the ashes back to Connecticut. But anywhere in France is okay with me."

"I would prefer to have her here," he said decisively. "And with a plaque, so I would know she was here."

"I, too, Mother," said Debby; "I would like it here, if it were possible, but somewhere else if necessary, with a marker, so there would be a place I could come to and it would say ABIGAIL GORHAM."

Her face was swollen with tears. I looked at both of them.

"See what you can do, Jean," I agreed. "But don't be too disappointed. Wherever it is, we'll share the cost; remember, we'll share the marker. Half and half, yes?"

"I, too," said Debby. "I want to share it too. It's for me, too."

We drove halfway down the hill and went into the church. It felt comfortable and cool inside. It was a church in use, old though it was. The light streamed in, warming the stone. There were notices of meetings and pamphlets on the table. One was called *The Young Catholic Wife*, and there was another one on Catholic education. It was an austere, simple, peopled church, beautiful and spare. I remembered how Van Gogh had painted it, the outside view of the apse against a nervous purply sky. Yes, I thought, Abby would like to be near this too.

Above the Rue Gachet ("Gachet!" I thought. "All of these mementoes of the painter's France") we found a little workmen's café with a patch of green under a tree in front. There was a table and chairs. We had a drink of bottled lemonade, chemical but cool. Then we drove back to Paris. It was dinnertime, our last night in France. Jean drove us to the Parc de Montsouris, looking for another restaurant that he and Abby had loved, but it, too, was closed. He turned the car back toward Montparnasse and brought us to the *brasserie* of the Closerie des Lilas.

I looked at him gratefully. The Closerie. Only last month Abby had sent me a letter about it. Her square, precise handwriting flashed through my mind. I could see her words. "Had dinner at the Closerie des Lilas last night and I thought of you and the first time I had dinner there with you and how you shortened my dress in the hotel room so I would be in style, do you remember? Anyway, it has now become very in to go to the bar and they have a sort of bar menu for the new crowd. It was really quite fun."

The next morning, Jean arrived early to drive us to the Charles de Gaulle Airport. As we followed the road, buses, taxis, trucks crowding us, I thought, how can we leave him? He is part of us. I had never seen him until last week. I would never forget him now.

"Do you mind if I play?" he asked, reaching for the tapes.

"Please," Debby and I both said. "Yes."

"What?" he asked.

"Play that same Dylan for me and the other one for Mother. Which do you prefer, Jean?"

He shook his head. "They are both Abby's. Her music. I'll play them both."

So first there was Dylan and then Simon and Garfunkel, and as Jean took the turns that brought us to the TWA departure door, the music of "Silence" was not yet finished.

"Please," I put my hand over his to stop him from switching it off as we arrived. "Let it go to the end." So we sat at the curb until the record ended, and again my face was clammy with tears.

Jean put our luggage into a cart and then stood to say good-by. "I can't leave the car too long, it's illegal," he explained.

Debby embraced him and he held her close. I embraced him and said, as I had before, "Thank you, Jean. I would have understood if you had not been able to care for us this week."

His eyes widened in question.

I kissed him again. "If you had simply disappeared," I explained.

"But it is normal, what I did," he said, using the word normal in the French way—appropriate, acceptable, expectable. "How could I have done otherwise?"

We saw him draw away in his car, waving at us from the window, and I thought, "My dearest, darling Abby, good-by."

## Some  Postscripts

Abigail Gorham, born December 23, 1943 in New York, died August 4, 1976, in France, is buried in the cemetery at Auvers-sur-Oise, above the church and across the field where the crows fly.


There are in the making a printed catalogue of her last paintings and drawings, and plans for an exhibition in France as well as one in the United States.


Her working notebook will be shown in a future exhibition of artists' notebooks and workbooks curated by Jacki Apple of the Franklin Furnace Archives, in New York.


Of the many letters from her friends, I want to quote from two:

*"Je ne peux oublier Abigail. Elle était pour moi la beauté et l'intelligence. Une nuit me promenant avec elle dans les rues de Paris, je l'ai vue auréolée, éblouissante d'une beauté ne lui appartenant (déjà) plus, faisant partie de la vie même. Elle m'a révélé subitement ce que la beauté a d'éter-*

*nel. Je ne peux oublier son rire. Et toute l'intelligence, la lucidité qu'elle était. Je la garde en moi. . . ."*

And from another:

*". . . nous tous ici, malgré la douleur . . . nous vous envions beaucoup d'être la mère d'Abigail. . . ."*

Which, in other words, says:

". . . all of us here, in spite of the grief, envy you deeply for having been Abigail's mother. . . ."